THE SOCIALKIND APPROACH

*We are committed to reducing our environmental impact, which is why our books
are printed on certified paper from sustainably managed forests (FSC, PEFC).
But we have also decided to take things a step further by taking the radical decision
to only print "on-demand". This means the book you are holding was printed individually.
It was printed only once it had been ordered by your favorite bookshop, by yourself
or by someone you know. This same principle holds true for all of the books we publish.
We therefore have no extra stocks, no unsold copies, no wasteful transport costs,
no paper sent to landfill. We align our publishing with the quantities ordered by
our readers, thereby minimizing our environmental impact.
This process of course implies a somewhat complex organizational
structure, marginally higher production costs and slightly longer delivery
dates, but we believe these are truly worth the returns.*

Lexitis Éditions

19 rue Larrey – 75005 Paris – www.LexitisEditions.fr

Delphine LANG

THE
SOCIALKIND
APPROACH

LEXITIS
éditions

TURN YOUR BUSINESS INTO A RELATIONAL BRAND

**BE AMONG THE BRANDS
THAT COUNT MOST
IN THE DAILY LIVES
OF YOUR CONNECTED CUSTOMERS.**

Delphine Lang

WWW.DELPHINELANG.COM

About the author

Delphine Lang is a social media expert, strategy consultant and trainer. Her mission is to break with the traditional codes of social media marketing and to go beyond received ideas by making the art of effectively managing one's social media activities accessible and comprehensible for everyone.

After more than a decade of working in well-known companies, both for corporates and advertising agencies, she decided in 2014 to explore her interest in the relationships between brands and consumers.

In 2016, she redefined the codes of social media marketing by unveiling her innovative approach, called "the SocialKind approach", to enable companies to achieve genuine operational excellence and, as committed actors, to actively participate in creating a better, safer, more just and more humane world for current and future generations.

Today, she promotes change by providing professionals with valuable insights and guidance resolutely focused on the acquisition of new skills and the adoption of new mindsets, behaviors and practices, in order to better respond to the ever-increasing expectations and requirements of consumers and to make a real difference in a constantly changing, and more and more complex and competitive world.

Introduction —————————————————— 15

Part I
Your quest ————————————————— 19

Part II
My philosophy ————————————— 23

Part III
Context————————————————— 27

I.   Social media that has changed the rules of the game ———— 27
II. Consumers who behave and consume differently ———— 28
III. Companies that act and sell identically ———— 34
IV. An unequal power relationship———————— 38
V.   The problem: the lack of understanding and skills———— 39

Part IV
Action ————————————————— 49

I.   Commit to innovative growth strategies ———— 50
II. The solution: the SocialKind approach ———— 52

A. Turn your business into a relational brand ———— 53

1. Respond to higher-order consumer needs ———— 53
2. Offer an experience focused on the brand's
symbolic dimension ———————————— 58
3. Build sustainable relationships founded on trust
and reciprocity———————————— 61
B. Build solid foundations to master your social
media presence ———————————— 63

1. How to think: lay the 7 pillars of an ideal culture ———————— 66

Pillar #01: responsibility ——————————————————— 66
Pillar #02: engagement ——————————————————— 68
Pillar #03: collaboration ——————————————————— 69
Pillar #04: risk-taking ——————————————————— 70
Pillar #05: innovation ——————————————————— 72
Pillar #06: optimization ——————————————————— 72
Pillar #07: optimism ——————————————————— 74

2. How to behave: build a powerful strategy in 10 steps ————— 74

Step #01: clearly define your brand identity ————————— 75
Step #02: precisely set your objectives ————————— 77
Step #03: conduct a precise analysis of the competition ————— 79
Step #04: acquire an in-depth understanding of your customers— 80
Step #05: draw up a consistent offer that meets the demand ——— 85
Step #06: set up your pages and accounts on the
            appropriate channels ————————————— 91
Step #07: define key themes and create optimized content———— 92
Step #08: establish an editorial calendar ————————— 102
Step #09: implement a database of customer knowledge———— 104
Step #10: measure your performance and adjust your strategy —— 110

3. How to act: adopt the 12 fundamental best practices _____ 112

Practice #01: use the codes specific to social media _____ 112
Practice #02: publish regularly and at the right time _____ 113
Practice #03: ensure constant monitoring _____ 115
Practice #04: deal with all requests _____ 117
Practice #05: listen attentively and empathetically _____ 118
Practice #06: respond quickly _____ 119
Practice #07: participate in discussions _____ 122
Practice #08: provide guidance and direction _____ 124
Practice #09: demonstrate transparency and sincerity _____ 125
Practice #10: calm things down and use private messages _____ 126
Practice #11: solicit influencers _____ 128
Practice #12: reward loyalty at two levels _____ 131

Part V

Results _____ 133

I.   Maximize your impact, your power of influence
      and your performance _____ 133
II.   Measure your social ROI with relevance and reliability ____ 134

A. Current measuring practices _____ 135
B. Why change _____ 136
C. The SocialKind philosophy on the social ROI
    measurement _____ 142

III. Leverage trust-based relationships
      with your influencers _____ 144

Acknowledgments _____ 153
Selective bibliography _____ 157

Being present on social media platforms with the aim of engaging consumers with published content without knowing how to use them effectively is like putting oneself at the controls of a plane to fly passengers to their final destination without knowing the flight plan. Do not take this risk. Take control of your social media activities with comprehensive knowledge and full understanding of the direction to take.

Delphine LANG

Before diving into the heart of the matter, some clarifications need to be made. The first concerns the difference between the terms "social media" and "social networks".

Social media generally refers to all the web sites and platforms which offer Internet users "social" functionalities – creation and sharing of content, exchanges between users, etc. – and enable one to create social networks, that is, communities of members (individuals or organizations) sharing common areas of interest and connected to each other through links. The nature of the links that exist between members of a network depends on the social networking site: Facebook friends, Twitter and Instagram followers, YouTube and Pinterest subscribers, etc.

In common usage, we have a tendency to use the term "social media" to refer to the ensemble of editorial sites (websites and blogs) which give the opportunity to create and develop social interactions. Increasingly since 2009, we have also tended to use the term "social media" to talk about "social networks", which is to say sites specifically designed to enable the creation and development of communities by their users through a social media platform.

In this book, in line with common usage, I will use the terms "social media" and "social networks" largely interchangeably to refer to these platforms.

Another important observation for those who might not be familiar with the term "engagement". The company that seeks to engage its customers with the content it publishes on its pages, accounts and/or channels seeks to make them react, meaning to make them like, comment and/or share its posts.

Furthermore, whether your company markets products and/or services, I will only mention the term "products" – and not "products and/or services" – to simplify things and to facilitate reading.

Finally, I am addressing myself to any company, and more precisely to any person who manages a brand, whether directly or indirectly, depending on his or her position in the company. Whether you are an advertiser, an agency[1], a not-for-profit association, a politician, a celebrity, an influencer, etc., this book was made for you.

---

1. Managing the social media presence of brands on behalf of business customers.

The SocialKind approach

Introduction

All companies and brand managers[2] have one day or another dreamed of discovering the formula that would enable them to guarantee the success and profitability of their social media activities. Today indispensable to any good communication strategy, social media is exceptionally powerful. Nevertheless, it is essential to use it effectively in order to avoid allocating time and mobilizing financial and human resources in vain. Not to mention the extremely negative impact on the image of the brand and on the growth of the company in the case of ill-adapted use.

When communicating with customers through social media, there are many factors to be taken into account to make the published content sufficiently attractive, captivating and convincing to motivate consumers to engage. That is why having a solid, clear and coherent social media strategy is indispensable for any company wishing to act advisedly.

Defining one's brand identity, setting one's objectives, clarifying one's mission, as well as acquiring a deeper understanding of one's customers, are key steps that must be taken to guarantee the engagement of one's community and make one's social media presence profitable.

Today, it is no longer enough to talk about oneself – whether in relation to one's company, brand and/or products – nor to increase the visibility of one's content through ad campaigns, to guarantee the success

---

2. Community managers in general, but these may be other employees in the company who take on community management functions.

and profitability of one's activities. Extolling one's merits to consumers is no longer enough. Rather, it is a question of offering a consistent and unique experience that strikes an appropriate balance between useful and enriching solutions, to meet the needs and expectations of one's customers. In other words, one's value must be proved through one's actions – by providing oneself the means to carry them out – which goes well beyond more communication of information about one's products.

In an ever-evolving environment where competition is always intensifying, the ability to offer a differentiated, high value-added "customer experience" to connected consumers is the guarantee of the success of a company, in any field. This requires a constant commitment to striving for excellence in order to provide an impeccable service that meets the growing requirements of consumers.

Instead of seeking profitability at any cost, companies should consider it not as an objective in itself, but rather as an outcome of their actions. An outcome of the excellence of their know-how and their "know-how-to-be" on social media. An outcome of useful and meaningful actions. Actions in line with the needs and expectations of their customers whom they are dedicated to indulge. Actions that are really effective in seducing and engaging them.

Given the ever-expanding use of social media, companies have more means and opportunities than ever to build privileged relationships with their customers. The channels are multiplying, as are the points of contact and interaction, communities are flourishing everywhere... And yet today, still too few companies are using social media in a well-adapted manner, missing what really matters to achieve the desired results.

Although many companies claim to place not the brand but the customer at the heart of their thinking process, this does not translate into practice. As a sign of a clear position based on a logic of communication of information about their products rather than that of a useful and enriching experience, the way they currently act on social media platforms does not reflect a customer-centric approach.

Because they are not given an offer which creates sustainable value for them, connected consumers do not feel sufficiently understood by the companies and brands they follow and with whom they attempt to communicate. There is therefore a long way to go for companies to show that they are up to the challenge.

Social media is a place for every kind of debate. These days, "it's where it's all happening". Expanding into these realms is to risk finding one's customers in a very different state of mind from the one that companies are used to dealing with.

Consumers today are increasingly demanding, and the communication actions companies consider relevant on social media do not necessarily – or rarely – have any value in their eyes. This is a worrying fact that hinders well-being and development on the side of both companies and consumers.

With millions of individuals around the world connecting every day, it is in companies' best interests to use social media "differently", more effectively and more creatively, if they want to avoid missing out on the innumerable riches, as yet unexplored and untapped, that social media has to offer. This necessarily requires changing the way in which they think, behave and act, by integrating technologies into an intelligent strategy.

This book provides you with the full equipment you need to benefit both from a deep understanding of the need for change – in the interest of all – and from a comprehensive knowledge of the innovative growth strategies to put in place in order to achieve genuine operational excellence and a significant competitive advantage.

You will then be able to ensure the growth, development and control of your social media activities, made possible by a perfect mastery of the indispensable elements required to steer them with complete autonomy and confidence.

Part I
Your quest

The main goal of any company, regardless of its field of activity, is to make profits, and this by selling its products.

According to the majority of companies present on social media platforms, their main goal is to engage their customers, current and potential, and this by communicating about their products.

But what does engagement, in the true sense of the word, actually mean?

> An engaged customer is a satisfied customer.
> An engaged customer is a consumer of the content that a company spreads through social media and traditional media and/or a buyer of its products.
> An engaged customer is a loyal customer.
> Engaged customers are loyal customers.
> Loyal customers translate into a rise in profits.
> A rise in profits results in company growth.

It is therefore in proposing an offer that fully satisfies consumers – in other words, in behaving "as they should" – that companies can succeed in engaging them. And thus achieve their goal.

The question to ask is this: in their quest to engage their customers, are companies present on social media platforms adopting the right attitude?

To engage connected consumers and maximize their chances of success, they produce content and invest more and more human and financial resources.

In this way, they ensure for themselves a certain return on investment: more fans, more followers, more likes, more comments, more shares and more views of their posts. However, many of them deplore the fact that they do not achieve the desired results. Trapped between the expectations of immediate results and the constraint of paying more and more to guarantee the engagement of their audience, they continue to make unfavorable strategic decisions with a view to boosting their performance and ensuring their development. By continually repeating the same mistakes, they can only achieve limited results across the board.

The attitude adopted by most companies clearly shows an evident lack of knowledge and understanding of the rules of the game of supply and demand played on social media, as well as what is at stake in the relationship to be built and developed with the connected consumers of today.

Overwhelmed by their day-to-day tasks, many of them appear not to envision a change to their approach, and rather persist with the one they have always used. No questioning planned for the time being. However, it is not the lack of time that explains the lack of sustainable returns, but rather the lack of direction and control over their activities.

Is it not time to change the tune and stop hoping, in vain, for better results by continuing to act in the same way? Is it not time to restore the fundamental goal of any business – to make profits – as the absolute priority?

To achieve one's goals, one must, above all else, know how. Do you want to know how? Do you really want to? Then continue reading this book, and you will know. Knowledge that will prove extremely powerful in comparison to that those who prefer to wait for "the day when..." The day when it will be too late, because they will be overrun by the change-makers. The leading companies of tomorrow of which you will surely be one if you go to the end of the process and do what is necessary to fully exploit this valuable knowledge, this wealth that will be yours.

After an in-depth phase of observing the surrounding world, the time will come to break down the barriers that prevent one from tapping into the potential of digital technologies. The time to change the traditional, mistaken beliefs that can only lead to ill-adapted behavior and ineffective actions. The time to change your mindset, your behavior and your practices by expressing yourself and letting nothing stop you.

There is no limit. Only those one imposes on oneself. Everything is just a question of willingness and the desire to head in the right direction. Wanting to deviate from traditional, inefficient and relatively unproductive patterns, and making every effort to prepare oneself to make a difference. This certainly takes time, but isn't the most important thing to achieve your goal?

TURN YOUR BUSINESS INTO A RELATIONAL BRAND

BE THE CHANGE
YOU WANT TO SEE
IN YOUR CUSTOMERS' ATTITUDE
TO YOUR BUSINESS.

Delphine Lang

WWW.DELPHINELANG.COM

Part II
My philosophy

The way companies carry out their digital activities is not a plucked from the air: it is the result of an accumulation of beliefs and rules peddled and transmitted since the emergence of social media.

Companies base their approach on the way they were taught to conceive of social media. They cannot do otherwise because they do not know "how to do things differently". They have their own limits: the limits imposed on them.

If I point out that their attitude is paradoxical, someone might say to me that it is the same in every company. I grant you this, and you might well also think so. One should certainly not believe that "in other companies, things are better".

Throughout my professional career, working for various companies, I had few reference points outside the limited world that was the corporate environment in which I pursued my path and tried to carve out a place for myself. Everything I was told was supposed to be treated as the absolute truth. My superiors in the hierarchy advocated certain beliefs and rules, explicit or implicit, that determined their own behavior and were meant to dictate the behavior of everyone. Norms that one must certainly not call into question.

By observing and analyzing the consequences of this common course of conduct, I nevertheless very quickly came to think that these beliefs and rules were illogical, incoherent and absurd. The outcomes resulting from the way we behaved and acted were frequently far too unsatisfactory for me to accept what was dictated to me. But in a system – the business environment – where conformity is law, and driven by the desire to fit into this little world, the one which society wanted me to conform to, I had to comply. I could not escape it.

At least, that is what I believed for a long time. That is until recently, when my determination to change what must be changed and the force of my convictions pushed me to develop my thoughts and refine my vision, to reach the final stage I had set for myself: to precisely define how to think, behave and act differently. More effectively and more creatively.

The right mindset, the right behavior and the right practices: I have identified and formulated them clearly. All this represents a powerful force for me, but most importantly for you, because my intention is to share this knowledge with as many people as possible in order to lead the change that is required and which we all wish for, at company level as well as individual and societal levels.

Convincing connected consumers of today to engage in a relationship with you through your brand requires a relevant and coherent approach in order to guarantee the quality, effectiveness, and profitability of your social media activities. In part IV, you will discover *The SocialKind Strategic Blueprint*: the strategic model that I created and that explains, step by step, how to command a powerful and effective social media presence and thereby succeed in the digital transformation of your company. In addition to the "how" to use social media differently from traditional use that is currently made, my approach emphasizes the importance of "why" change without delay. In the following part of this book (part III), I will give you all the elements that will enable you to solve the enigma of the digital transformation that everyone is talking about, tracking it to its source, that is to say by understanding all the circumstances that justify the adoption of a new approach.

It is clear that the companies with the greatest chance of success are those that are ready to call into question the beliefs and rules they blindly follow and change what must obviously be changed in order to provide their customers with the best possible offer that rises to their expectations and requirements.

Now it turns to me to convince you to be one of them and to give you the solution that will enable you to achieve this goal.

TURN YOUR BUSINESS INTO A RELATIONAL BRAND

YOU DON'T HAVE TO BE THE LEADER

IN YOUR FIELD

TO POSITION YOURSELF

AS A MUST-HAVE BRAND

IN THE EYES OF YOUR CONNECTED CUSTOMERS.

Delphine Lang

WWW.DELPHINELANG.COM

Part III

Context

Ever-greater consumer requirements, combined with the growing competitiveness of the environment and the constantly changing technological evolution, oblige you to know and truly understand the rules of the game of supply and demand that operates on social media, in order to avoid basing your decisions on obsolete assumptions.

What is needed is to clearly identify the rules, sort the misconceptions from the reality, and bring tangible proof of what connected consumers of today expect from companies and brands on social media.

This step is essential to understanding the need to leave behind a traditional approach in favor of a new one, in order to generate significantly more value from your activities as well as to get a step ahead of your competitors.

I. Social media that has changed the rules of the game

Previously, there were two coexisting channels of contact: points of sale and the online sales catalogue. In the absence of platforms for direct exchange between consumers and companies, the dialogue was mainly one-way. Companies launched trends and consumers had no choice but to adapt to them. The rules of the game undeniably favored companies to the detriment of consumers.

In the past decades, two channels of communication have become increasingly important: web and mobile. Used separately by companies, until recently they responded to consumers' expectations. Companies still had a certain amount of leeway.

The emergence and expansion of social media brought these two parties, namely the companies and the consumers, considerably closer together by offering the latter unprecedented power of freedom of expression.

Today more than ever, consumers can make their voices heard much more strongly. And they do not hold back. Whether it is to share their point of view, their opinions and their concerns or to request information from a company, responses to their questions and solutions to their problems, their voices are heard more and more, in all generations and in all sectors.

The control of the relationship between the two parties has consequently evolved and changed hands over time. An unquestionable transfer of power in favor of consumers. Nowadays, consumers very often launch trends. It is the companies' turn to adapt.

II. Consumers who behave and consume differently

Formerly passive, consumers have become real actors in the marketplace, active and involved, and from the youngest age. Observing even the smallest companies' actions, they easily master the exceptional tool that is social media. In their daily life, they combine the advantages of the digital and the real world and shake up entire sections of the economy on digital platforms (websites, social networks, blogs, etc.).

Given the growing use of technology, their consumption patterns have changed. In the past, one consumed according to necessity. Today, the simple search for possession of material goods appears to be over.

Consuming is no longer enough. Consumers do not let themselves be as easily seduced as before, except by the companies who know how to talk to them. Companies that have taken the time to really understand them and prove it through actions that are useful and meaningful in the eyes of their customers.

But who are these "new-generation" consumers?

Constantly connected, they have completely integrated new technologies into their lives. They show their ability to consume digital content actively, intelligently, in a creative and engaged way. They play with the complementarity of social media and other channels of communication with total ease. With disconcerting aptitude, young children, although they sometimes do not even yet know how to write, have already entirely understood how to use their parents' tablets – if indeed they do not have their own.

Consumers today are more and more autonomous and informed. They know how to demystify consumer codes and make use of spaces of expression other than those of brands. In the past, they asked their inner circle, whether friends or family, before making a purchase. Although that is still true, they now favor the opinions of other consumers – often perfect strangers – from social networks, blogs, and online comparison sites. Sources of information and advice that they perceive as trustworthy and objective.

They have never been so influential. Social media are places for discussion and debate where consumers spend time expressing their opinions on a diverse array of subjects: a news event, the latest escapades of a celebrity, the release of a new product, etc. They also use them to share their customer experiences, give their opinions after a purchase and share their tips and make known the deals they have found, as well as find out about ones from others. For those who are truly active and engaged in the creation and the sharing of content – many users are rather passive, limiting themselves to watching what is being circulated on the web – they embody true brand ambassadors on the web and social media, without companies ever having to call on them to take on that role. The exploding popularity of fashion bloggers who share their advice daily with their thousands or even millions of fans and followers is the perfect example. Some of them have become true stars of the digital ecosystem in a very short time. Key influencers for brands, being very few in number and highly sought-after, who distinguish themselves from brand ambassadors by their very large audience and their power of influence, which is often more significant than that of celebrities who have taken years to build their reputation. An undeniable power they exercise in exchange for payment, free products, invitations to private sales, etc. This is a phenomenon which is becoming more and more important, leading many companies to call on the most influential bloggers of the moment to represent their brand and extoll the merits of their products.

They judge by comparison. With a plethora of sources of inspiration and information at their disposal, they can make sound decisions on a brand without its intervention. They decide to buy after having compared the offers proposed by different brands, and this after having explored the web and collected opinions from all sides. The messages coming from companies now represent only one source of information among a wide range of options.

They are more and more fickle. They no longer hesitate to change brands when they are unsatisfied, if the company has not been able to hold their attention, keep its promises and meet their expectations, or quite simply if there is a better offer elsewhere. They decide where, when and how to consume.

More and more adept at one-click shopping, they no longer hesitate to make their purchases on the Internet, from their computer, their smartphone or their tablet, making their choices via search engines without paying attention to the marketing messages carefully designed by brands.

Many of them prefer e-commerce to going into a store for certain types of purchases (clothing, food, leisure activities, etc.).

Mobile technology has radically changed the way they buy. On the move and armed with their smartphone, they now have a very precise idea of what they are looking for when they arrive at a point of sale.

They are more impatient than ever. Always in a rush, they no longer tolerate waiting. They want to be able to make their purchases quickly, when they want, without putting up with the never-ending line at store cash registers.

Given the plethora of promotions that they see in their news feeds when they connect to the various social networking sites, connected consumers have a tendency to buy more than non-connected con-sumers. They are bigger spenders because they are more tempted... They are also easier to retain, though this does not necessarily mean that they are "more loyal". Quite the contrary, given the breadth of the choices offered to them, regardless of the type of products they are looking for.

Digital has deepened the relationships between companies and con-sumers, but it has also contributed to raising the level of expectations of the latter. More and more disposed to doing research on the Inter-net before making a purchase, new-generation consumers are no longer satisfied with messages vaunting the merits of this or that prod-uct, nor those encouraging impulse purchases. Although this is what the current offer from most companies on social media is limited to, they expect to be offered much more than simply products.

Consumers – which we are, you and me – want more useful and meaningful content in regards to the choices and decisions they have to make. They expect companies not to consider them as mere buyers, but as individuals in their own right.

They are very clearly on a twofold quest.

On one hand, there is a search for useful solutions to save time and money, all while expending as little of their energy as possible. In search of what is best for them, they expect brands to act as real advisors.

On the other hand, they are looking for enriching solutions, for pleasure, to lead a dynamic life, rich in entertainment and amusement. Seeking to live new emotions every day, they expect brands to bring them a part of the dream, and the emotional content that will appeal to their senses.

In this twofold quest, they have very specific expectations when they connect to social networking sites. Expectations that can be categorized as rational or emotional.

Rational expectations

In their search for useful solutions, they expect to:

– be given useful, practical and easy-to-understand content;
– get access to content quickly and easily;
– take advantage of exclusive, personalized and unique offers;
– be able to buy what interests them at any moment, through the channel of their choice;

– benefit from more responsive customer service than those on traditional channels of contact.

Emotional expectations

In their search for enriching solutions, they want to:

– interact when they want with their favorite brands and other Internet users;
– grow their network of relationships through new encounters;
– experience strong emotions;
– be inspired;
– chill out.

Consumers want brands that no longer attempt to seduce them by displaying badges, logos, and status symbols, but rather that appeal to their senses and spark the pleasure of listening to what they have to say in pressing their emotional buttons.

If one compares the way consumers of yesterday and of today make their food purchases, one might say to oneself that their behaviors and buying habits have radically changed. Previously, they never hesitated to spend hours, totally relaxed, in supermarkets to do their weekly shopping. Nowadays, though they still go to stores regularly, new-generation consumers turn more and more towards the Internet. Seeking to optimize their resources – in terms of time, money and energy – they have an unlimited choice, and the feeling of total liberty that digital platforms provide in terms of the decisions they have to make is exactly what they are looking for.

Does this mean that consumers plan to go to physical points of sale less and less? Very clearly, no. In the case of supermarkets, one can easily see that many of them do not pay attention to the time when they find themselves in chains that provide them with a complete offer, distinguishing themselves in this way from what they might find elsewhere. Chains that have supplemented their basic offer – mainly food products – with services of all kinds, but especially with sections entirely dedicated to leisure, in which consumers can find products they do not necessarily need but that they desire (multimedia, gardening supplies, decorations, etc.). Chains that, in this way, allow their customers to combine the useful with the enjoyable: doing their shopping while experiencing pleasure!

Consumers therefore firmly choose to dedicate time where they have an interest, that is to say, where they perceive value.

This is an observation that is valid no matter what the channel of contact, including social media.

But companies must have integrated this and act accordingly to provide their connected customers with what they are looking for.

III. Companies that act and sell identically

On social media, companies are constantly seeking the right strategy to make themselves indispensable to the members of their online community. What is the dominant approach? How are companies operating?

Regardless of whether a brand's social media presence is managed within the company that owns it or entrusted to an agency, content is created to promote its products. If it has a communication plan covering the launch of new products, events or any other business transaction currently in progress or to come, the posts are created on the basis of this plan. If the company does not have a communication plan, content is produced on the basis of what there is to communicate on at the time. In both cases, the goal is clear: to engage.

In order for posts to be seen by the target audience, there is little or no alternative – according to received wisdom – than to pay to increase their visibility. The choice of the type of ad campaign is made according to the underlying objective: an increase in the number of fans or followers, the number of likes, the number of comments, the number of shares or the number of views. From the moment the content is published on one or more platforms, the company has little left to do but sit back and wait for things to take shape... Yet perhaps this is not exactly right. For example, in the case of a recruitment campaign on Facebook[3], the company must choose, when planning the campaign, the level of budget to be allocated among different possible options. For each level, it can see the number of new fans that it will have at the end of its campaign. It has only to choose the option corresponding to the desired results... and pay for it.

In the short term, the company gets what has been promised: visibility for its posts and new fans joining its community by liking its page. But in the long term, there are no guarantees. So if the link created with these new members who have interacted with its brand during the campaign is not nurtured over time, these hard-won fans will have no interest whatsoever in the company. Whether they are potential customers or fake fans – individuals who are paid to react to the brand pages and posts of brands or who do so merely to boost their own visibility on platforms – they will very quickly break the link with the brand, by simply unliking[4] its page, because the brand has done nothing to nurture and strengthen it.

Such an approach does admittedly lead to positive results. For the span of a campaign. However, to succeed on social media, it is not a question

---

3. An ad campaign that seeks to recruit fans for its Facebook page.
4. Removing the "Like" which they had previously given.

of creating value over a certain period of time, but rather of creating value both today and tomorrow.

The sequence of actions and campaigns, which reveals both an obvious lack of a clear and coherent strategy and a short-term vision, does not in any way allow the company either to generate concrete and sustainable benefits or to ensure its growth and development. Driven by the will to make profits in the short term, it finds itself acting on all fronts, with no specific direction. The results are indisputable: shrinking communities on certain platforms, low or even inexistent activity levels and engagement levels that are too often limited.

An approach which does not allow the company to convert individuals who follow it through social media into engaged and loyal customers. It does ensure, in the long term, a growth in turnover thanks to an increase in its sales, whether in stores or on its e-commerce site.

This approach, which clearly focuses on the communication of information about company's products, is more about mere presence rather than real engagement aimed at immersing the customer in a high value-added experience at the heart of the brand. Knowing that consumers are willing to buy more products from the same brand on the condition that the offer they are provided with fulfills their needs, responds to their expectations and gives them the feeling of being able to choose without excessive pressure, simply limiting oneself to vaunting the merits of one's products is completely counter-productive.

This traditional approach, followed by the majority of companies today, certainly does not allow them to build strong and sustainable relationships with their customers, but rather turns them away...

An approach that is now obsolete.

TURN YOUR BUSINESS INTO A RELATIONAL BRAND

WHAT MONEY CAN BUY:
VIEWS, LIKES, FANS.
WHAT MONEY CAN'T BUY:
TRUST, LOVE, LOYALTY.

Delphine Lang

WWW.DELPHINELANG.COM

IV. An unequal power relationship

In many companies, the power relationship plays out at two levels: on one hand, between the company and current or potential customers, and, on the other hand – for those who outsource customer relationship management – between themselves and the agencies which manage their social media activities. Ideally, both levels should be complementary and support each other symbiotically. In reality, the power relationship is unbalanced. At both levels.

In their relationship with the consumers they address, companies clearly demonstrate as much a lack of knowledge and understanding of the new challenges in "customer relationship management" as of the way to use social media effectively to reap the full benefit. By basing their approach on a logic of communication of information about their products, they indeed do not demonstrate the ability to give their customers what they are asking for, both in terms of customer experience and service. They are faced with consumers who have fully integrated the potential offered by social media in terms of closeness, sharing and dialogue. Consumers who master the use of these communication tools, which they very often use on a daily basis.

In their relationship with the agencies – for those companies who entrust these latter with the keys of the management of relationships with their customers – the fact that they do not have the same expertise as their interlocutors in terms of community management[5] translates into a lack of confidence which leads them to follow the recommendations which they are given in terms of the traditional approach, since nothing else is proposed. They find themselves dealing with agencies which, in some cases, lack strategic thinking and long-term vision –

---

5. Management of a brand's social media presence..

something which they acknowledge themselves, and indeed more and more of them are demonstrating their needs in terms of strategic skills. Their offer is very often built around the combination of "content and performance". The production of content combined with the amplification of its visibility through advertising campaigns in order to ensure a certain level of performance, in the short term, of their operations. Content strategies, creating little or no sustainable value.

This twofold power relationship in no way serves the economic interest of companies, nor does it allowing to satisfy consumers.

V. The problem: the lack of understanding and skills

81% of companies claim that they have a good understanding of their customers. Among consumers, only 37% consider that their favorite brands understand them, and that number dips to 22% for brands in general[6] (the term "brand" is more appropriate from a consumer perspective, since it is with brands that consumers connect and interact on social media).

If one listens to the individuals to whom they address themselves, true understanding by companies of what consumers expect from is limited, or even nonexistent.

Companies clearly misunderstand the needs and expectations of connected consumers as well as those of their customers in general. Powerful knowledge, necessary and indispensable to give themselves the means to succeed, and which is worryingly lacking among most of them.

---

6. Cf. bibliography, n. 1.

And yet the expectations of companies are quite similar to those of their customers, namely:

WHAT COMPANIES EXPECT FROM CUSTOMERS	WHAT CUSTOMERS EXPECT FROM COMPANIES
Attention when they communicate	Attention when they express themselves
Reactions to their actions	Reactions to their requests
Participation in their campaigns	Participation in their discussions
Engagement	Engagement
Loyalty	Rewards for their loyalty
Interest in their products	Interest in their needs and expectations
That they consume their offer	That they respond to their demand

It is a mistake to think that keeping one's promise and communicating on the quality and functionalities of one's products is enough to succeed in engaging connected consumers. This is the most basic politeness, indispensable to being on social media, but it is not enough to succeed. Nevertheless, many companies think that it is.

A satisfied customer who has everything he or she was promised at product level can leave and break the link that ties him or her to the brand through social media simply because he or she is offered something better elsewhere. It is not the fulfillment of the promise that strengthens or weakens customer loyalty, but the very nature of the promise that is being made.

Unsatisfied customers turn away from a brand primarily due to a bad "customer experience", and only secondarily because of a weak "product promise". The two variables in the acquisition and retention of a customer are the product and the experience. As for price, that only has little influence. Companies that think that the price of their products will help them build a competitive advantage and that it plays a major role in influencing consumers in their favor may suffer serious disappointment.

If one considers customers who leave for another brand because of a promise of a richer experience and/or a superior product promise, one might logically think that the new offer corresponds more to their needs and expectations than the first one that was proposed to them. And thus that it results from a better understanding by this brand of their needs and expectations.

Considering the customer – and not the brand – as the "hero" and placing him or her at the center of one's communication is crucial to developing a reassuring discourse, which is in turn key in an uncertain world where individuals feel less and less secure. That said, when one knows the real cost of creating a 360° view of the customer, one should not be surprised that the majority of companies have advanced so little. To do so indeed requires a certain amount of investment both in terms of time and research, which very few companies up to now have been ready to dedicate.

When companies do not understand them, consumers choose the least bad offer. Depending on whether one considers the glass half empty or half full, one could either say the situation is disastrous or, on the contrary, that there are golden opportunities for those who make progress in the areas of their knowledge and understanding of the customers they aim to engage on social media. Companies that will thus give themselves the means to draw up and propose an offer that lives up the demand of their customers.

The ill-adapted behavior of companies on social media platforms can also be explained by the fact that a good number of them rush onto them in no particular direction. Only 15% of companies in the first stages of digital maturity and less than 50% of those in development – which is more than seven companies out of ten – possess a clear and consistent strategy[7]. Absence of strategy means absence of a mission and clearly defined objectives, and poorly adapted – therefore inefficient – use of the tools they handle.

Furthermore, fewer than half of companies are aware of the previous purchases made by their customers online. There are also very few that capture and/or exploit data related to their offline interactions, which reveals a total lack of consistency in the customer experience, both online and offline, throughout the buying process.

By relying on various data to evaluate the performance of their activities, companies nevertheless get the impression that they are progressing if their number of fans or interactions (likes, comments and/or shares) with their posts is on the rise. Yet these data, generally taken from the platforms themselves or specific monitoring tools, are for the most part absolute values that give no indication of what really matters to evaluate their return on investment effectively. They are figures that do not allow companies to evaluate to what extent their social media activities have contributed to the growth of their business, or to make sound, well-founded and relevant decisions on the way in which they can improve the effectiveness of their actions.

Paradoxically, companies continue to invest more and more resources, hoping thereby to achieve better results.

---

7. Cf. bibliography, n.2.

The SocialKind approach

In short, there is considerable scope for improvement by companies, including the most popular ones, in the digital realm. Still today, many of them are missing what really matters, and due to a lack of knowledge and understanding, are incapable of exploiting the full potential of all the growth opportunities afforded by social media. However, the greater the savviness of the customer, the greater the likelihood of missing the boat.

Companies that in the past held all the cards and that did not pay sufficient attention to the needs and expectations of customers must now imperatively take them into account, not to mention the changes in consumer behavior. This taking into account is of the utmost importance and must generate major modifications in both their own attitude and their offer.

For the majority of companies, responsibility for the management of their social media presence is very often entrusted to young people, who are constantly connected for their non-professional activities. However, a command of these tools for personal use in no way guarantees the ability to manage a brand's presence effectively. And there is truly an important gap between the way in which people interact casually with other individuals in their personal life and the way in which they manage the interactions with their customers of their company in a professional context.

Knowing how to use these tools effectively to manage a brand's presence requires strong skills and very specific knowledge, which a good number of these people do not have, whether or not they have certificates or diplomas testifying to their aptitude in community management. The reason? What is taught at schools and universities are the traditional beliefs and rules, passed down since the emergence of social media, without any questioning of their relevance. Norms which lead companies to adopt ill-adapted behavior. Norms which have become obsolete and which must be changed by integrating the reality of today.

A brief aside... I know that I am upsetting the apple cart by saying such things, but given the argument of the ineffectiveness of these norms with regard to the current performance of the social media activities of many companies, which themselves express a real uncertainty about the effectiveness and profitability of their actions, my goal is indeed the following: to raise awareness in order to make all the difference by bringing a solution to the problem, in the interest of both companies and consumers... That being said, let's move on.

Being aware of one's skills gap and giving oneself the means to fill them equates to giving oneself every chance to master the art of conducting one's activities and guaranteeing their success and profitability. Knowing how to rapidly adapt to changes in the environment and propose a consistent offer, designed to respond to the ever-growing expectations and requirements of consumers, is proving to be an important ability, much more important than technological skills. This inevitably requires an understanding of the surrounding environment in order to embrace change and lay within the company the fundamental pillars needed to grow together – the company, its employees and its customers.

Given the obvious benefit of using social media beyond simply communicating information about their products, companies must find a way of playing their cards well in order not to find themselves in a position where they are losing complete control of the "customer relationship".

Right now, this is far from being the case. Very few companies are giving themselves the means to obtain the skills needed to genuinely exploit the full potential of social media. Companies that will continue to undermine their efforts – until something is undertaken from the ground up to change what needs to be changed and show that they are up to the challenge.

The need to change their approach, indispensable for success, forces company executives, whether they like it or not, to ensure that their internal teams have the necessary skills to guarantee the effectiveness of their social media activities. It is essential to develop a genuine internal strike force by disseminating as widely as possible the knowledge required to skillfully pilot one's social media presence.

These days, many organizations provide training in community management. Many company executives send their staff to such courses, convinced that their employees will then have acquired the knowledge required to manage their social media presence in the right way. However, these training sessions, which are also passing down the traditional beliefs and rules, unfortunately do not help executives to create value either for their company or for their customers.

What is required is to acquire real strategic thinking and adopt an innovative approach, which cannot be transmitted through the courses currently available on the market.

Company executives have every interest in changing their approach and embracing change if they do not want to continue hoping, in vain, for better results from their activities.

Some executives will commit to the path of change in order to reinvent themselves and to significantly increase their position as preferred partners in the eyes of their customers and thus increase their turnover. Others will try to maintain their position they have achieved – a cautious attitude, common among companies, due to a lack of confidence in the face of the evolution of technologies and their uses.

All this will undoubtedly shuffle the cards, but one thing is sure: companies which provide themselves, without delay, with the full equipment needed to achieve genuine operational excellence and develop their capacity to seduce, convince and retain their customers will have a major competitive advantage over those who delay the acquisition of the knowledge and skills indispensable for success.

The full equipment you need you are holding in your hands.

To make the change that is needed, you have to know how. There's no need to search around anymore... the solution is here.

TURN YOUR BUSINESS INTO A RELATIONAL BRAND

BECOME A MASTER OF THE ART OF SERVING YOUR CONNECTED CUSTOMERS WITH EXCELLENCE.

Delphine Lang

WWW.DELPHINELANG.COM

Part IV

Action

In an environment where the struggle for visibility is fierce and where consumers are more and more demanding, getting closer to one's customers by adopting a differentiated approach which aims to offer them both useful and enriching solutions is the best way to stand out from the competition and win over as many people as possible. And it is precisely through social media that companies can become closer to their customers.

Succeeding in this challenge requires a radical change, which means engaging in the vast digital transformation movement, which concerns all companies, whatever their field of activity. Investing in change necessarily involves rebalancing the power relationship between companies and consumers. This has emerged as an unavoidable fact that is shaking up all companies, all over the world.

Making the choice to go through the process of digital transformation is a sensible decision, which companies must take if they want to give themselves every chance of success with the implementation of a genuine social media strategy. A strategy ensuring their growth and development. A strategy providing real added value for their customers. A strategy responding more widely to the concerns of our society.

Companies must, however, be aware that this transformation does not simply imply the digitization of their activities. It involves changing not only the state of mind of all their collaborators, the way in which they use social media to promote their products, but also the working methods within the organization in its entirety.

PART IV

Companies that have the best chance of succeeding are those that are prepared to question both common misconceptions and their beliefs about the use of social media, and to change their mindset, their behavior and their practices in order to respond in the best way to the needs and expectations of the consumers of today.

The choice is yours: play the game by the same rules or change your approach to shuffle the cards and rebalance the power relationship with your customers. Make the right choice, in the interest of all – your company, your employees, your shareholders, your customers and society as a whole.

Be aware, however, that between now and the moment at which you no longer have any choice but to change, it will be too late. Very often, you have to make the leap even before your collaborators feel ready to do so.

If you want to succeed in exploiting the full potential of countless riches offered by social media before others, make the choice to change. Right now.

I. Commit to innovative growth strategies

The capacity to rethink your business through a digital lens rests in large part on a powerful strategy, supported by company executives who foster a culture that encourages change in their mode of operations and their practices.

Digital transformation is not really a question of technology, but rather of strategy[8]. Indeed, unless owned by a company, a technology offers

---

8. Cf. bibliography, n.2.

no inherent competitive advantage[9]. The majority of technologies are accessible to anyone. The fact that a company expands into a social networking site such as Facebook or Instagram does not procure it any real advantage over its competitors, whether or not they use the technology concerned.

The trap to avoid is to bet on technology as an end in itself. Technology should rather be considered as a means of achieving the objectives of a powerful strategy. The majority of companies commit the error of focusing all their attention on technology at the expense of strategy. By resolutely emphasizing the operational dimension of their activities, they focus on solving specific problems related to technologies taken on a case-by-case basis.

Do not fall into this trap. Your strategy must be developed with a view of adopting new behavior on social media platforms, by using technology effectively in order to achieve your strategic objectives. Giving importance to using technology as of means of building on your image as an innovative company as well as improving your decision-making process will demonstrate the wide, ambitious vision for the future you aim to create, beyond the technology itself.

As you will have appreciated, in order to achieve the change that is needed on social media and to gain a competitive edge over your competitors, the step to take is to invest in an innovative growth strategy. This requires an investment on your end, which will be eminently worthwhile.

If you continue on the path I am inviting you on right to the end, it is a safe bet that you will be one of the leading companies in the eyes of

---

9. Cf. bibliography, n.3.

connected consumers, regardless of whether or not you are a leader in your field of activity in terms of size or market share.

II. The solution: the SocialKind approach

Offering genuine opportunities for growth and a major competitive advantage, strategies based on the SocialKind approach which I have elaborated aim to maximize the level of closeness between consumers and companies, through the adoption, by the latter, of an innovative, bold and visionary attitude. An attitude which leads them to act as providers of useful and enriching solutions. An attitude which clearly aims at positioning themselves as essential partners in the lives of their customers.

The fundamental principle of the approach is to become a relational brand.

A brand capable of winning over the hearts and minds of its customers.

A brand capable of convincing them of its value and the necessity of its products.

A brand which embodies strength and longevity.

The underlying idea is that individuals choose consumer goods as much for their utility functions as for their symbolic ones. Thus, they favor brands and products the representations of which meet their sophisticated needs – the satisfaction of primary needs being a necessary and indispensable prerequisite – and fulfill their expectations.

In view of the behavior of the next-generation consumers, embodying a relational brand is without a doubt the best way to distinguish yourself from your competitors and to win over your public, whatever the field of activity.

A. Turn your business into a relational brand

By deploying your activity on social networks, your goal must remain the same as the one you have probably already set for yourself: to engage. What needs to be changed is how you achieve that.

The way you operate must be effective and efficient. In other words, it must first and foremost serve the interests of your customers and allow you to reach the primary goal of any business: to generate profits.

If you succeed in meeting the needs and expectations of your customers in a meaningful way, using smart communication and proposing an appropriate offer, your communication efforts will be greatly eased. Such an offer, which will win over the consumers you seek to get engaged, will require less commercial pressure, which will subsequently allow you to reduce your promotion costs and, in the end, increase your profit margin.

There are three essential directions to follow.

1. Respond to higher-order consumer needs

The pre-existence of a need in consumers with which the products of a business are concerned is essential for considering design its offer.

Often one hears talk of "creating a need". This expression is erroneous. Marketing does not create needs, it only reveals them.

In reference to Maslow's hierarchy, needs, which are classed into five stages by order of importance, pre-exist in every human being: from primary, lower-order needs, which are physiological needs and safety needs, to sophisticated, higher-order needs, which are belonging needs, esteem needs and self-actualization needs.

Lower-order needs #01: physiological needs

Directly linked to ensuring survival, physiological needs (eating, drinking, dressing, etc.) are the most dominant needs of an individual. These are concrete needs that one can easily associate with the need to consume.

It is obvious that the need to consume in and of itself is not sufficient to justify the existence of the plethora of products available in a variety of sectors, such as fashion, food, interior design, telephony or automotive. The explanation is elsewhere.

One product can meet several needs: for example, a car can be used to get around, to save time or to display one's social status. Ultimately, many types of vehicles may correspond to the list of specifications expressed in terms of needs. But it is the response to his or her expectations (design, comfort, additional features, etc.) that very often leads the consumer to make a particular decision. In this way, although the universal rule for private car use is ownership, other customer segments can be identified. Consumer groups that have a totally different conception of the car. It is no longer necessarily an object one owns and which conveys the image desired by the driver. For them, it is more a question of convenience. There is a shift from the notion of possession to the notion of use, which implies a different conception of the use of a car and which forces the market players to rethink their offer.

Informing one's customers about one's products constitutes the basic principle of communication, whatever the channel of communication used, including social media. It is nothing more than responding to the physiological needs of the individual. Needs that are fundamental, essential, "obvious". Not fulfilling these needs will have an inevitable impact on the other needs.

Lower-order needs #02: safety needs

Safety needs are the result of the individual's aspiration for feeling protected both physically and psychologically. Meeting safety needs alleviates the individual's concerns and fears. A feeling of strength and control over his or her world is then generated[10].

As a social media user and in his or her relationship with a brand – regardless of the products it offers – these safety needs mainly manifest themselves in a desire to live a coherent, unified and ongoing experience. The more these needs are left unsatisfied, the more this will push the individual, in search of a feeling of safety, to turn to another brand which will satisfy him or her.

The feeling of being protected physically and psychologically is built during childhood, through the assurance of parental protection and from the feeling of safety felt by the parenting couple towards life itself. If this feeling is not experienced by the individual, he or she may perceive the surrounding world as hostile and threatening.

As a company, it is by teaching the individual the rituals and rules specific to its brand that it will help him or her to organize and bring stability into his or her world.

Starting from the principle that satisfying the needs of one stage gives rise to the needs of the next stage, sophisticated needs are triggered only when physiological needs are met and safety needs are relatively fulfilled.

---

10. Cf. bibliography n.4.

To become a relational brand, beyond the satisfaction of your consumers' primary needs in terms of the communication of information about your products, you must aim to fulfill all of their other needs. Making a difference in this way will unquestionably allow you to win over your public.

Higher-order needs #01: belonging needs

Belonging needs correspond to the need to love and be loved, the need to have friends and the need to belong to a peer group. In the event these needs are unmet, the individual experiences a thirst for relationships and belonging to a group, whether social, personal or in terms of status – each individual can belong to several groups. Hence the importance, largely underestimated by the majority of companies, of considering connected consumers not as mere buyers, but rather as individuals belonging to their brand's network.

Exchanges through social media should generate much richer contact opportunities between a brand, whatever it is, and its customers. They must allow the individual to strengthen his or her sense of belonging to a community of members sharing the same values, the same interests and the same passions. The company must help him or her become part of the group united around its brand and identify with it and all that it symbolizes. The brand must represent a point of reference. A proof of belonging to a relatively exclusive club uniting "people like me".

Higher-order needs #02: esteem needs

Esteem needs correspond to the desire felt by any individual for a sense of self-confidence. The need for positive esteem for oneself and from others, as well as the need for respect for oneself and from others.

On one hand, esteem needs encompass the aspiration to power, performance, attention, importance and appreciation, and, on the other hand, the aspiration for renown or prestige, recognition, confidence in relation to the world, independence and freedom.

If these needs are unmet, the individual experiences feelings of inferiority, weakness and powerlessness. It goes without saying that a brand which incites such feelings will not win him or her over, and he or she will turn away from it very quickly.

On the contrary, if they are fulfilled, the individual will have feelings of confidence, personal worth, competence and power, in short of being useful in the world. These are feelings that any brand must make him or her experience in order to be recognized, respected and chosen.

Higher-order needs #03: self-actualization

Self-actualization needs correspond to the need felt by the human being to realize his or her potential, exploit and make the most of his or her potential in all areas of his or her life.

If the other needs are common to all individuals, the need for self-actualization varies greatly from person to person. During the course of one's life, everyone discovers where one's competencies lie and what one truly aspires to. And everyone has a different conception of how to achieve great things in one's life and make it worthwhile.

The individual fluctuates between imitation – in order to be accepted into a peer group – and differentiation – in order to affirm his or her identity. To be accepted by the group to which he or she belongs, the manner of expressing his or her differentiation to the group must be expressed through brands which respect the "codes" of the group. And once they have been accepted, brands and products, which, if they are new, can allow it to evolve.

The adherence to a brand represents a non-verbal way for the individual to express his or her vision of the world and feelings, and make his or her preferences known. With respect to the rules of the consumers they are addressing, the brand must enable the individual both to affirm his or her personality and distinguish himself or herself without overly standing out.

Distinguishing oneself is one of the most common traits of individuals who socialize extensively through social media. This characteristic is reflected in the need to conquer.

The adherence to a brand then becomes an art of conquest of "the other", the group or the society as a whole.

2. Offer an experience focused on the brand's symbolic dimension

In the past, the symbolic dimension played a minor role as to whether a consumer chose a product or not. These days, it plays an essential role because it is the symbolic dimension which guides the act of purchasing and consumption in general.

The utilitarian, material value of a brand is in the inherent quality of its products, their uniqueness, their functionalities, their finishing, etc. These criteria of material quality vary by product. Another important element has to do with points of contact with customers, which contribute to reinforcing this value if they are of high quality.

The symbolic, non-material value of a brand is in the image created around its products, which help define its unique positioning compared to its competitors, and thereby what the brand represents in the eyes of consumers. These can have two distinct opinions on two brands offering exactly the same product, simply because of the differences in terms of brand image.

TURN YOUR BUSINESS INTO A RELATIONAL BRAND

THE CLIENT COMES FOR THE PRODUCT.
HE STAYS FOR THE EXPERIENCE.

Delphine Lang

WWW.DELPHINELANG.COM

From our adolescence onwards, we are all compelled to endure strong social pressures that make us sensitive and receptive to the symbols inherent in consumer goods. A phenomenon which has grown considerably over the last few decades.

Teenage culture, with its norms, values, attitudes and practices, is recognized and shared by young people. It is represented by a multitude of symbols and common meanings. Through the interpretation of these codes, adolescents give their opinions and pass judgments on others, based on, for example, the clothing and accessories brands they wear. Being accepted by a peer group often depends on wearing the right brand of jeans or tennis shoes. Not wearing the right brand can result purely and simply in being excluded from the group.

Whether adolescents or adults, individuals in our contemporary civilization consume "symbol" more than ever. Beyond their utilitarian value, brands are more and more recognized and consumed for their strong symbolic value.

Symbolic consumption is based on the principle that individuals, depending on situations, have a tendency to consume products or specific brands both in order to show a certain image of themselves and to identify with a peer group. Through their possessions, they seek to express their identity just as much as they seek to achieve social recognition.

Turning towards consumer goods in relation to the messages they want to convey to others, their choices depend on what they think brands or products will symbolically communicate to others about their individuality. They take into consideration the whole set of images and ideas related to the brands, and more particularly the symbolic benefits. These benefits are the most extrinsic advantages of the consumption of each of the brands that are in close relation to their higher-order needs. What consumers think a brand will give them socially will have a major impact on their consumption choices.

On the basis of this principle, the brand must be symbolically important in all the actions it undertakes on social media platforms in order to stand out from others and to win over customers. It must allow customers both to manage their identity through a process of identification with a group united around it, and to benefit from a certain recognition within the group and society as a whole. In short, it must represent a benchmark, a guide, with values that are stable and recognizable to all, so that every individual may evolve, grow and "be" within society.

3. Build sustainable relationships founded on trust and reciprocity

The main factor determining the loyalty of a customer is trust. Consumers are ready – and even prefer – to buy more products from the same brand once they trust it, which requires an enhancement of the brand's involvement with its customers. A mutual commitment. A reciprocal exchange which will encourage their loyalty.

The overall satisfaction of a customer and the quality of the contact that he or she has with a brand throughout the entire customer lifecycle significantly influences his or her loyalty. Making this cycle as rich as possible and providing the best service when a problem arises both allow, then, the brand to secure their loyalty. This is why recognizing the importance of the customer relationship is key, both at the time of sale as well as throughout the entire customer lifecycle, which is to say before and after the act of purchase.

The company must do everything in its power to meet every last desire of its customers, current and potential, by continuously adapting to the evolution of their needs and expectations. This inevitably requires understanding the reasons why they are or might be possibly willing to put an end to the link that unites them with the brand on social media.

It is by actively engaging with connected customers and by doing everything necessary to prove its engagement that a brand can succeed in converting them into valuable allies.

Once they trust a brand, customers – often those who are already active on social media platforms – can become major spokespeople, by supplying social media (social networks, blogs, forums, etc.) with increasingly positive recommendations about the brand and products of the company that was able to earn their trust. Among these highly engaged customers who trust a brand and make it known, some may exercise a considerable power to influence the consumption choices of other Internet users. These are commonly referred to as "brand ambassadors".

Whether mass consumption products or luxury items, media, a personality or an association are in question, this concerns them all. Indeed, what better selection criterion for a "brand" – the examples cited above are all to be considered as such – than the recommendation from a customer who testifies to the trust they have in a brand by openly talking about it on social media? The answer: none.

Brand ambassadors play a key role at three levels:

- They act as intermediaries in creating a relationship between the brand and new customers.

- They nurture the relationship between the brand and its newly acquired or less loyal customers.

- Through their involvement, they reinforce the relationship that they themselves have with the brand.

They bring a real contribution in various areas:

1. Visibility: given that a potential buyer generally needs to be exposed to a brand's advertising message three to five times before being convinced of buying its products, he or she will be more quickly motivated to move on to the act of purchase if he or she receives positive messages from other customers about the brand's products that he or she is considering buying.

2. Credibility: being consumers themselves of the brand's products, recommendations coming from them are without a doubt the most credible form of advertisement.

3. Trust: when a consumer has to form an opinion about a brand or its products, trust is much higher in other consumers' opinions than any other kind of information or advertising.

4. Engagement: consumers who purchase on the Internet spend more after having received recommendations from other Internet users who have already experienced the brand's products.

In essence, long-term trust-based relationships mean sustainable and profitable growth. As a consequence, building, maintaining and strengthening trust-based relationships with its customers through social media is for any company the absolute guarantee of optimizing its return on investment and of creating long-term value for all actors involved.

B. Build solid foundations to master your social media presence

The success of your social media activities depends on the acquisition of knowledge and skills indispensable to providing your customers with an offer that perfectly meets their demand.

Through the adoption of an innovative, relevant and consistent approach which goes well beyond the traditional approach adopted by the majority of companies present on social media platforms these days, you will succeed in standing out from the competition and positioning yourself as the preferred partner of your customers.

After setting out the fundamental principles of the SocialKind approach, I now invite you to discover all the components of this approach through *The SocialKind Strategic Blueprint:* a comprehensive and detailed guide, which I have developed for you, and which explains, step by step, everything you need to know to adopt it as quickly and as effectively as possible.

As mentioned earlier, following the SocialKind approach, the phenomenon of the digital transformation of your company means turning your business into a relational brand, which implies a scenario of rupture.

This scenario plays out in three phases:

1. Change your way of thinking through the transformation of your company's culture.

2. Change your way of behaving through the drawing up of a powerful strategy.

3. Change your way of acting through the adoption of fundamental best practices.

Here is the comprehensive and detailed roadmap.

THE SOCIALKIND STRATEGIC BLUEPRINT	
HOW TO THINK: LAY THE 7 PILLARS OF AN IDEAL CULTURE	
Pillar #01	Responsibility
Pillar #02	Engagement
Pillar #03	Collaboration
Pillar #04	Risk-taking
Pillar #05	Innovation
Pillar #06	Optimization
Pillar #07	Optimism
HOW TO BEHAVE: BUILD A POWERFUL STRATEGY IN 10 STEPS	
Step #01	Clearly define your brand identity
Step #02	Precisely set your objectives
Step #03	Conduct a precise analysis of the competition
Step #04	Acquire an in-depth understanding of your customers
Step #05	Draw up a consistent offer that meets the demand
Step #06	Set up your pages and accounts on the appropriate channels
Step #07	Define key themes and create optimized content
Step #08	Establish an editorial calendar
Step #09	Implement a database of customer knowledge
Step #10	Measure your performance and adjust your strategy
HOW TO ACT: ADOPT THE 12 FUNDAMENTAL BEST PRACTICES	
Practice #01	Use the codes specific to social media
Practice #02	Publish regularly and at the right time
Practice #03	Ensure constant monitoring
Practice #04	Deal with all requests
Practice #05	Listen attentively and empathetically
Practice #06	Respond quickly
Practice #07	Participate in discussions
Practice #08	Provide guidance and direction
Practice #09	Demonstrate transparency and sincerity
Practice #10	Calm things down and use private messages
Practice #11	Solicit influencers
Practice #12	Reward loyalty at two levels

1. How to think: lay the 7 pillars of an ideal culture

Companies that engage in a transformation process in their activities often focus on obtaining an immediate return on investment without thinking more long term, and in particular without considering that their collaborators (employees, shareholders, external partners, etc.) may not be ready to accept change. However, the involvement of everyone and the synergy between the different departments of a company are essential prerequisites to the success of any change.

Laying the pillars of a new approach within the company, mobilizing all collaborators so that they can accept change and ensuring their commitment allows you to solidify your position as a relational brand and your brand's appeal among consumers. This requires putting one's collaborators into a shared "customer-oriented" culture, understood and integrated by everyone, in order to encourage organizational, individual and social development.

A culture fostering change and innovation is the hallmark of leading companies.
Such a corporate culture is built on seven key values that help ensure successful change: responsibility, engagement, collaboration, risk-taking, innovation, optimization and optimism.

Pillar #01: responsibility

Distinguishing yourself through your sense of responsibility, taking concrete actions and persevering in your activity in order to achieve excellence guarantees the growth and development of any company.

To make sure every collaborator feels responsible, individually and collectively, and for him or her to motivate others to do the same, self-esteem is an indispensable prerequisite.

The feeling that the company in which the collaborator exercises a "function" and has a role to play shows esteem for who he or she is and what he or she does, and that it consistently treats him or her with fairness and consideration, elicits the intrinsic motivation of every collaborator and encourages the fulfillment of his or her responsibilities.

Referring back to Maslow's hierarchy of needs, every collaborator must experience four distinct and complementary feelings so that he or she feels responsible, both individually and collectively.

A sense of security

Setting clear and precise objectives, establishing effective procedures and calling on the engagement of the entire workforce gives each collaborator a stronger sense of security, which is fundamental to a state of well-being.

A sense of identity

The individual and unique style that each employee possesses is a precious source of innovation and change.
The company must respect its collaborators in their differences, lead them to be conscious of their qualities and strengths, as well much as know and recognize those of others, in order to create a climate of confidence allowing each individual to freely reaffirm him- or herself.

A sense of belonging

Involving the entire workforce and informing all collaborators about the company's social media activities gives every employee the opportunity to feel like he or she belongs to a group with common objectives. This is a necessary and sufficient motivation for everyone to endorse the collective mission, vision and values of the company.

A sense of skill

The company must give its collaborators the resources needed to develop their skills, so that they are ready to meet both personal and shared challenges.

Pillar #02: engagement

As a point of reference regarding the success of its activities, engagement of all the company's collaborators is one of the keys to the success of any digital transformation. It is thanks to the involvement of all that the company can succeed in traversing change and ensure progress.

Given that individuals are only interested in changing only when they perceive and understand the reason for doing so, deliberate measures must be taken to provoke and stimulate the engagement of all collaborators, no matter how many there are.

Company executives must imperatively ensure they acquire the required resources needed to develop the digital skills and know-how of their employees, as well as their own. A better knowledge at all levels of the company will lead to increased engagement and stronger participation among all collaborators, regardless of their position within the company (executive, brand manager, press officer, in-store salesperson, etc.).

This increased engagement of executives with respect to their collaborators will also reduce the risk of losing them. Indeed, these days, employees of all ages wish to work for companies that are deeply engaged in a digital process. This sentiment is felt across all age groups, to a nearly identical degree.

The commonly held belief that digital technology is "the business of younger generations" is completely false. On social media, it is all about interactions between humans – which is not a domain limited to the "Millennial generation". Having full command of technology on behalf of your company is the kind of knowledge that can be acquired at any age, whether you are 25 or 55.

Pillar #03: collaboration

Companies too rarely provide their employees with a collaborative working environment that stimulates individual and organizational development. As products and economic models are becoming increasingly complex, companies are creating a growing number of silos[11] in order to make the management of their organization easier. This is especially the case for large companies.

This simplified management structure erodes innovation. It in no way encourages members of the company to share their knowledge with others, to learn from others and help others, nor to gain from each other's experiences.

The creation of collaborative working styles is the key driver for innovation. The success of a digital transformation depends on the collaboration between the different departments and collaborators of the company. From this collaboration depends the effective implementation of an "omnichannel" strategy, where all of the channels of contact between the company and its customers are used and exploited simultaneously and collectively, as well as the satisfaction of customers through the different channels of communication.

---

11. This signifies that each company department of the company works relatively or totally independently with respect to other departments.

Certain channels of contact with customers should not be exclusive to one department in particular. Each department must be aware of what is happening within other company departments. Sharing information about current and upcoming actions and campaigns, whether on social media or traditional media, as well as sharing data related to customer knowledge that are exploited by each department, is essential in order to make sure that all collaborators have a clear view of the activities of the company in its whole.

In companies where each department works in isolation, the implementation of a social media strategy must go hand in hand with leaving their culture of working in silos behind, in favor of adopting collaborative working methods. It is this transition to greater collaboration that will ensure the success of their strategy. Without this, it is doomed to failure.

Furthermore, executives should encourage the cohesion of their workforce by encouraging unity within diversity. Integrating their collaborators into cross-functional teams with various kinds of knowledge and know-how gives them the possibility of working with other groups on the implementation of initiatives that are sources of innovation.

Supplying the required resources to get individuals from different backgrounds to participate in the realization of diverse and varied projects unquestionably contributes to guaranteeing the success of the company's activities over the long term.

Pillar #04: risk-taking

Transformation means taking risks. In search for new forms of competitive advantage, companies that engage in the process of the digital transformation of their activities by acquiring the full equipment needed to reach their destination are more at ease with risk-taking than those which have not yet started out. They master what must be done and are conscious that taking risks is indispensable to move ahead and impress their customers through an offer that ceaselessly adapts to their expectations and requirements.

Taking risks necessarily implies the possibility of failure. In order to stimulate risk-taking within their company, executives who are risk averse must force themselves to change their mindset. Even at the risk of failing – after all nothing in life is guaranteed – they should not stop themselves from daring to act. If their attempts end in failure, they should consider this failure as a step towards future successes, all the while learning from their errors in order to do better the next time.

Executives must also consider the possibility that their collaborators may be resistant to taking risks. If this is the case, it is their responsibility to motivate them to be more daring.

Aversion to risk constitutes a serious obstacle which prevents many companies from progressing. Choosing to play their cards safe, they tend to run away from risk, which prevents them from exploring new opportunities.

Developing a culture less adverse to risk is in no way an insurmountable task. Daring to take risks requires being fully aware of the fact that change is an absolute necessity for ensuring the growth and development of one's company.

Today, the costs of inaction virtually surpass the costs of action. It is therefore better to act at the risk of making mistakes, than to do nothing at the risk of not progressing and never achieving the success one desires.

Pillar #05: innovation

Transforming the culture of one's company translates into the necessity of adopting a culture built on innovation and creativity. A culture which cannot be dissociated from an approach that aims to offer a useful and enriching experience to one's customers. This gives the company the capacity to rapidly and effortlessly incorporate the changes to be made in a continuous way.

It is a common belief that innovation or creativity emanates from the flashes of genius of a limited number of individuals who possess a special gift. In reality, many brilliant new ideas come from the collaboration between individuals from different backgrounds. Bringing people of different backgrounds and points of view together is both enlightening and extremely valuable for the growth and development of the company.

Pillar #06: optimization

Putting oneself into test-and-learn mode[12], using one's own experience and drawing inspiration from the experience of others, enables one to develop one's abilities with the constant aim of progression and evolution.

Learning from one's mistakes, doing everything in one's power not to repeat them while improving what needs to be improved, questioning oneself and accepting criticism, identifying new opportunities and continuously adjusting one's actions leads to generating concrete benefits from one's social media activities, since the company is constantly ensuring that its offer is entirely consistent with its customers' wishes.

---

12. The "test-and-learn" mode consists of experimenting with solutions and new modes of functioning to learn from and optimize your activities depending on the achieved results.

The SocialKind approach

**SUCCESSFUL BUSINESSES
SEEK TO BUILD COMMUNITIES.
ALL OTHER BUSINESSES
SEEK TO SELL PRODUCTS.**

Delphine Lang

Pillar #07: optimism

Striving to have a positive influence on one's environment by engaging one's collaborators in a common and interdependent movement in order to build trust-based relationships with one's customers demonstrates the quality of the company's engagement and its long-term vision.

The company must believe in change, in progress and in its capacity to contribute to a better world in order to guarantee the well-being and fulfillment of current and future generations.

Collaborators must position themselves in a state of mind that brings together optimism and realism. Being capable of seeing the positive side of things helps to reduce the tension that surfaces when a problem arises considerably and helps to avoid becoming preoccupied with events over which one has no control.

Furthermore, the common way of thinking must remain grounded in the human dimension, tolerance and non-judgment. This is first of all and above all what consumers expect from brands in their interactions through social media. This way of thinking should lead collaborators to respect the specific situation of each person and to believe that, whatever happens, situations – even annoying ones – should end positively. Taking initiatives to find appropriate solutions to problems that are met unquestionably helps earn public trust.

2. How to behave: build a powerful strategy in 10 steps

It is by providing an exceptional offer that constantly provokes consumers' desire to engage with your content and consume your products that you will succeed in building, maintaining and strengthening trust-based relationships with your customers. Consequently, you will be able to ensure sustainable and profitable growth for your company.

To arrive at your destination, you have to know the direction to take, which you can only find by having a comprehensive and detailed roadmap. In other words, drawing up a coherent and convincing strategy that will allow you to make the value of the relationship with your brand obvious in the eyes of your customers is a fundamental step in guaranteeing an optimal return on your investment.

The ultimate power of strategies based on the SocialKind approach lies in their scope, their clarity and their uniqueness.

There are ten steps to follow.

Step #01: clearly define your brand identity

In an extremely competitive world and facing consumers that need, more than ever, tangible proof of the true value of a brand, you must be sure to establish a clear position in the minds of your customers by bringing yourself as close as possible to the identity symbolism they are looking for.

Social media platforms have so many pages and accounts that a brand identity which is not clear or too out of sync with the expectations of its customers will very rapidly fall into the abyss.

The notion of brand identity still remains far too underutilized by companies in their social media activities. However, it constitutes the basis and the unifying factor of all of the manifestations of a brand.

The name and logo of a brand does not only represent the visible side of a much more complex reality. These signs ensure the mediation between, on the one hand, the image that a brand projects through the values it conveys and, on the other hand, the perception that consumers have of the brand. If there exist "richer" brands than others, it is because they benefit from an evocative potential that is more powerful and more easily mobilized.

The experience that you will propose to your customers must send out powerful brand codes, so that they can create an image of your brand that is authentic and desirable.

To prevent the content that you publish from serving the interests of your competitors and to ensure that your customers immediately recognize that it comes from you, your brand universe must be unique. This requires defining what constitutes its uniqueness and clarifying your vision and values. The goal of such a clarification – or the definition if you have not yet defined it in your marketing plan – is to affirm them in all of the expressions of your brand on social media. And, of course, everywhere else as well.

Another element that constitutes the identity of a brand is its mission: the future direction of a company through its brand. It makes no sense to expand into social media platforms without having defined why to be there and what to do. Yet many companies present on social media show, in practice, that they have not defined a particular mission, other than that of informing their customers about their products.

The mission of a company through its social media activities represents a strategic element that is key to its success and gives it a major competitive advantage. To benefit, state clearly what the role of your company is in regards to your connected customers and what you commit to do for them by being present on social media platforms.

At this stage, the goal is to position your brand and products as the ideal solution in the eyes of your customers, current (retention and loyalty) and potential (recruitment). Imagine consumers in the quest for something quite specific: it could be to buy clothes or a car, get tips to learn how to apply makeup or decorate a living room, book a vacation, lose weight, etc. In their quest, your offer has to embody THE solution among the many offers provided by brands active on social media platforms. It has to stand out from the competition thanks to its unique and strong brand identity, which must be felt through all of your actions.

A quick aside: we generally speak about resolving a "problem" and presenting oneself as a solution to the customer's problem. In my opinion, this term is not appropriate because thankfully the customer is not always faced with problems needing to be solved! When the consumer is looking for credit because of a lack of cash, he or she is definitely faced with a problem that he or she is looking to solve by obtaining credit. But in the case of a consumer searching for a new watch, a beauty product or even a good vacation deal, we cannot truly speak of a "problem"... Talking about problems is a well-known habit in our society. In my view, it is high time to change this negative way of thinking about things, and to talk about a "quest" rather than a problem. A much more positive way of understanding the situation of the consumers one is looking to seduce and convince.

That being said, in order to encourage your customers to react, the identity of your brand must be attractive. It must also be credible, which means that once engaged you have to continuously keep your promise. Your brand identity must also be sustainable, as nothing is more ineffective than changing one's discourse from one day to the next. Once it is clearly defined, your mission will greatly facilitate the task of creating content to publish on social media (step 7).

Step #02: precisely set your objectives

Not defining the objectives you want to reach nor the expected outcomes clearly results in an incapacity to measure the impact of your social media activities. Conversely, being precise in the definition of your objectives will simplify the planning and the prioritization of the actions to be taken to reach them.

As there is no strategic model that suits all companies – the one you will develop on the basis of the roadmap that you are discovering will truly be unique – there are also no "ideal" objectives that suit all actions or campaigns carried out on social media platforms. It is up to you to define yours based on the GOMR procedure that I have created and which covers the four fundamental elements that must be taken into consideration:

– Goal: define the intention of your campaign (for example, to seduce new customers);

– Objectives: list measurable objectives (for example, to reach a critical mass in audience size);

– Metrics: identify key performance indicators (for example, number of fans);

– Reference points: clarify levels of reference (for example, +3,000).

The clearer and more precise the objectives, the easier it will be for you to determine if you have reached them.

For each objective, stay focused on a limited number of metrics and class them in order of priority. This will ensure a rigor that is neither too restrictive nor too complex for the post-action or post-campaign measurement phase.

Step #03: conduct a precise analysis of the competition

Once you have precisely determined your brand identity and your objectives, you can go to the next step, which consists of identifying the competitors you must or want to know more about.

Determining the brands that you consider to be "competitors" on social media necessitates increasing your scope of observation beyond your own field of activity. These might be much fewer in number than your direct competitors – or different to them. Indeed, one of your competitors might be present in your market but not on social media platforms.

Once your competitors are clearly defined, you can start the process of competitive intelligence.

For that, you will need to respond to the following questions:

– What social media platforms are they present on?

– What is the size of their online community, in total and on each social media platform?

– What is their level of activity? Are they more active on some platforms than on others? If so, which ones?

– What is the level of engagement of their audience? What is the level of likes, comments and shares that they are able to generate from their posts?

– What types of content do they publish?

The interest of carrying out competitive intelligence is not with a view to reproducing what works, but rather to be aware of what is happening around you and the manner in which other actors are addressing their audience through social media. In fact, the same audience as yours with regards to the direct competitors that you will eventually have included in your analysis.

Many of your target customers very likely receive your competitors' messages in their news feeds. Knowing your competitors' practices will confirm your belief that you will succeed in standing out if and only if you distance yourself from the traditional patterns of communication that are adopted by most of them, precisely by not doing things like the rest.

Step #04: acquire an in-depth understanding of your customers

Every company designs products intended for customers. It is imperative, therefore, that they know beforehand what the latter are likely to consume, and what the motivations and factors are that guide their choices. Understanding the elements that drive a consumer to the act of purchase is a vital factor for the success of any offer a company makes through any channel of contact with its customers.

On social media, companies publish content designed to engage their customers, who are both social network users and consumers of the products of their brands. It is consequently essential to know first what the determining factors that incite customer engagement are, in order not to upset them with irrelevant initiatives, but rather to nourish interactions with content that they will enjoy consuming and sharing.

The act of engagement results from the combination of multiple factors that interact and result or fail to result in the choice of the current customer (retention or loyalty) or potential customer (recruitment) for one brand instead of another: these factors are linked to the expectations of consumers, but also to their sophisticated needs (addressed earlier and common to all humans), their values, their behaviors and their use of technology.

To analyze how and why consumers will or will not opt for an offer that is made for them as well as engage in the content that is proposed to them, it is necessary to realize that they have, as social media users, very specific expectations in regards to brands that they like and follow through the different platforms. Expectations that they express in a variety of ways.

Closer relationships

Closer relationships means more availability, more sincerity, more accessibility, more listening:

- More availability: favoring social media when they want to solicit brands because they have a problem or question or need more information, connected consumers expect companies to demonstrate immediate reactivity.

- More sincerity: the more sincere the relationships, the greater the possibility customers will feel a certain level of closeness with their favorite brands.

- More accessibility: they want to have access to information about the brands and products that they consume or have the intention of consuming everywhere and all the time.

- More listening: they expect companies to pay attention to their reactions. If they express themselves – and this is what companies want – they expect, in return, to be listened to and understood.

More personalized relationships

Consumers would be more motivated by and engaged with content published by companies if the latter showed a better understanding for them by providing offers perfectly matching their specific characteristics: their expectations, their needs, their values, their interests outside of media, etc.

More human relationships

Individuals, as consumers, want companies to play the roles both as providers of solutions and as distillers of positive emotions. This is why they want peaceful relationships. Relationships that give them the possibility to learn and, above all, to entertain themselves. In short, to enrich themselves. They expect companies active on social media platforms to communicate in a less "administrative" way, that is to say that they adopt simple language, adapted to their codes, instead of looking to impress them with terms that they do not understand or master.

Connected customers also want their relationships with their favorite brands to participate in reinforcing their social connections and to contribute to the development of their community relationships. Consciously or unconsciously, they are looking to satisfy their need to belong to a community which shares common values, interests and passions.

Rewarded loyalty

Customers that are connected with the brands that they consume and buy products from expect to be rewarded for their loyalty at two levels: for their engagement with messages posted by brands on social media and for their consumption of products.

These four types of expectations, distinct and complementary, are not fulfilled by most brands that consumers connect with through social media. They represent golden opportunities for companies who know how to fulfill them. It is up to you to be one of them by taking the right actions thanks to the ideal approach that you are now discovering in order to exploit the full potential of its benefits.

In order to know the specific profile of your customers or different types of customers –according to criteria such as age or gender – as consumers of your products, do thorough research on the Internet. The web is a precious source of countless riches with regard to customer knowledge. In conducting your research, the goal is to find the answers to the following questions:

- What are their subjective and objective needs?

- What are their values, beliefs and feelings?

- What are their concerns? Their dreams?

- What are their behaviors?

- What are their expectations?

- What are their motivations?

- What media do they consume?

- What social networking sites do they connect to and which ones do they prefer?

- How many connected devices do they have? What do they use them for?

- How much time do they spend on them?

- What are they talking about?

- What are their activities outside of media?

- Where do they make their purchases?

To this non-exhaustive list, add every other question that you might find relevant to ensure in-depth knowledge and understanding of your customers.

With respect to notions of "needs" and "expectations", it is important to understand that the notion of individuals' expectations regarding consumption is subtler than that of needs, while being complementary. An individual might objectively need a product but might not be in the position of expecting it. Take for example a primary need: to clothe oneself. In his or her quest, an individual consumer is faced with unlimited choices, taking into account the considerable number of brands and styles of clothes that are available on the market. Once the purchases are made and his or her need is met, what explains whether he or she will be tempted to buy other items of clothing, assuming that he or she has bought everything he or she needed? The answer: desire.

The challenge that you must take on in order to encourage consumers searching for the products that you sell to choose yours consists therefore of provoking their interest and seducing them with a convincing offer and quality content, arousing the want and desire to possess your brand and your products rather than those of your competitors.

Step #05: draw up a consistent offer that meets the demand

Once you have acquired knowledge of the specific characteristics that drive your customers to engage and consume, the next step consists in drawing up your offer using all of the precious information collected. As we have just seen, it must be an offer that responds to or even provokes demand. An offer that will be considered by the consumers you are targeting as a real solution because you have taken their needs and expectations into account to draw it up. A unique, innovative offer. THE ideal solution that will enable you to stand out.

To become a relational brand and to make yourself powerfully connected to your customers, you have to prove the value of the relationship with your brand by making it comprehensible through the actions that you undertake on social media.

A unique experience

Starting with the assumption that we do not really know someone unless we know their story, if you want your customers to show interest in you it is important to tell your story.

The story is the main heritage of your brand. It is, most importantly, your best marketing tool. Everyone knows or can easily find out – via the multitude of available sources of information – what your products are, but not exactly what your story is. It is up to you to harness the wealth of your own richness to win over your public.

All great brands are those that, through their communications campaigns on traditional media, and, in some cases, also on the web, tell simple, magical, memorable stories that provoke the desire to immerse oneself in the brand's universe. This is precisely how you must seduce your customers.

Sharing one's history means much more than just posting fine words on the walls that are news feeds, but rather revealing the identity of your brand – your values, your vision and your mission – to your connected audience.

Define what makes you unique, your "one thing" that must be felt in all of the messages that you publish on social media platforms.

You have to create a discourse that belongs only to you, in connection with, on one hand, your brand, products and projects, and, on the other hand, the needs, expectations and desires of your customers. In other words, a smart discourse that says, in essence, "We know what you are like and we make available to you all the solutions that precisely correspond to your needs so you can make the best choices for yourself, by yourself."

A value-creating experience, intimately linked to your brand

Consuming a relational brand means consuming a product, a legend, a myth, a tradition, a know-how and the rituals of consumption. Unlike brands that present themselves more as products to sell, you must sell and offer for consumption all the dimensions of your brand.

The benefits that are expressed must be essentially emotional or even sensorial, and not rational.

To embody a relational brand in the eyes of the general public, your offer must essentially be designed around your brand and its symbols, rather than around your products themselves. From the storytelling of your products, you must move towards the collective building of your story, by plunging your customers into an experience that can be seen as an initiatory journey that will immerse them at the heart of your brand.

TURN YOUR BUSINESS INTO A RELATIONAL BRAND

IMMERSE YOUR CONNECTED CUSTOMERS IN A UNIQUE EXPERIENCE THEY WON'T FIND ANYWHERE ELSE.

Delphine Lang

WWW.DELPHINELANG.COM

One specific aspect of the symbolic consumption of brands is that it is strongly based on the similarity between self-image and brand image. The brand constitutes a means of expression for the individual who prefers a brand with an image that fits better with his or her own self-image, while the symbolic consumption of products is about the fit between the self-image and the image of the product.

Understanding this distinction will allow you to highlight, during the creation of your content (step 7), either the "products" aspect and their usefulness for your customers or the "brand" aspect and what it can offer them symbolically.

A luxury experience, combining useful and enriching solutions

As we have seen above, your offer must embody in the eyes of your customers, in search of a product that you provide, the best possible solution among all the offers available on social media.

On one hand, you must position yourself as a provider of useful solutions by helping your consumers in their search and allowing them, through your actions, to save time and money while expending the least amount of energy possible.

Share with them purchasing rituals and teach them rituals of consumption. Behaving like an advisor means never imposing, never telling them what they have to do, but rather making a proposal, by skillfully suggesting that your brand and products are what are best for them. In this way, you will succeed in being the first to come to their minds when they are ready to purchase.

On the other hand, knowing that the notion of pleasure is today becoming the primary motivation behind consumer purchases, you must act as a distiller of enriching solutions, rich in pleasure and enjoyment, in order to contribute, in your own way, to enriching peoples' lives. Confronted with the harsh reality of today, which is senseless and incomprehensible, individuals, in search of wellbeing, seek as much as possible to experience pleasure by using their senses, to entertain and to distract themselves in order to escape the dullness of everyday life. In this context, luxury is considered by consumers as a concentration of pleasure, an indulgence, a reward to oneself in a society that is more and more anxiety-inducing and less and less rewarding.

These days, luxury represents the dream and the excellence that individuals need. It is above all associated with personal pleasure, encouraging a feeling of belonging to an exclusive club, while allowing one to affirm one's identity. Luxury is thus fully anchored in a deep impulse in society today.

Whether your company markets luxury products or not, the purpose is to capitalize on the wider desire for luxury by moving away from the foundational codes of luxury, which are the exclusivity of the target, the selectivity of distribution and the discretion of communication.

The luxury experience to be offered to connected consumers must be perceived not as an ordinary experience for rich people, but rather as a rich experience for ordinary people. And therefore accessible to everyone of us on this earth. An experience intended for and accessible to everyone, all while providing the feeling that it is exclusive and reserved for exceptional individuals, which are your consumers seen through your brand.

The act of purchase must itself be a pleasure passing through emotion, the senses and the total experience lived, thanks to your brand, on social media and beyond.

A coherent experience

The coherence of the experience to be offered to your customers implies a relationship that is:

– fluid: clear and easy on different channels of contact;

– continuous: in real time and sustainable.

Everything must be accessible in an intuitive and almost instantaneous manner. Things must happen as though everything was thought of in order to make their search easier, to make it pleasant, and above all to prevent them from wasting their time unnecessarily.

Your customers must feel guided, oriented, served efficiently, to save them from any frustration.
Nothing must interfere with the attention of Internet users, aside from content, which must be simple to understand and to consume. The immersive experience must include everything your customers need. Nothing more, nothing less. It must also be as perfect as possible, sufficing by itself. They should say to themselves that there is nothing to add to or to take away.

"Less is more": making connected consumers whom you want to seduce and convince feel that they are in a privileged, exclusive universe that is reserved for them. The codes specific to your brand must be apparent or easily discernable.

An omnichannel experience, connected at each step of the customer journey

The multiplicity of channels of contact must not be treated like a stack of solutions proposed to customers on each channel considered individually.

The experience that you offer must be an "omnichannel" experience. A unified experience, identical no matter what channel of contact is used.

You must send the right messages at the right moments on the right channels in order to be in a position to provide the best relational experience before, during and after the act of purchase. Ensure, then, that the channels of contact that you have put or will put in place are used and mobilized in an optimized manner.

Step #06: set up your pages and accounts on the appropriate channels

For each type of consumer, there is a specific way of talking about a brand and its products, but also an ideal place for communicating and exchanging. The challenge that arises when the customer relationship is shifted to social media is to position oneself where customers find themselves on a daily basis.

Beyond building and developing relationships with one's customers, it is also a question of being in a situation of symmetry by using the same tools of communication. To maximize their engagement, engage in conversation where they most clearly spend their time interacting with brands and other Internet users. That is to say, where they feel the safest because they are on known, familiar ground.

Because you know which social networking sites they prefer (step 4), you will be able to prioritize your efforts and allocate your investments on the platforms that are most likely to produce the desired effects.

For each social media platform where you decide to set up – if you were not there until then – or to more strongly concentrate your activities, you must ensure that your page or account is optimized. This step is essentially operational.

Make sure the main information is there: name, description, contact information, links to your different pages and accounts on other platforms, links to your website, and other basic elements such as your profile picture, your cover photo, etc., in adapted formats according to the platform concerned. For the description to be included, clarify to your customers what your intentions are and what they can hope to receive from you on each social network. In other words, your promise.

If you have a Twitter account dedicated to customer service or if you intend to create one – Twitter being the ideal platform for online customer service – it is important to make it known to as many of your customers as possible, whether current or potential, and on different channels of contact. Add links on your website, your Facebook page, your main Twitter account, your LinkedIn page, in your newsletter, etc. If you have points of sale, make sure your salespeople talk about it to customers who walk through the door of your shops. This new-generation customer service is an asset to your brand. Make sure the maximum number of people are aware of its existence.

On the other platforms, it is a question of balancing the handling of requests expressed by your customers with the management of the customer relationship on the same page or account. The ideal is to lead your customers seeking assistance for a problem to get into the habit of contacting you on Twitter. However, keep in mind that many of them might still not be familiar with this social networking site.

Step #07: define key themes and create optimized content

Once you have defined your brand identity (step 1), including the mission that you will undertake to help your customers in their quest, and your strategic process, the challenge consists in making your customers understand that you are THE ideal solution, so that they will turn to you and choose your brand and products rather than others.

In order to succeed, you must affirm your identity and clearly explain it through high value-added content. Content that represents real solutions for your customers. These solutions must make them realize that in choosing your brand, their search is over because they will have found what they are looking for. From you.

Your solutions must both correspond to your objectives and offer value-added solutions to your customers. Far too many companies ignore the steps that consist in defining their objectives or knowing the profile of their target consumers. They go directly to the production of content meant to engage their audience, without any precise purpose or without any guarantee that it corresponds to what their customers are looking for. These are primary, fundamental errors, in the one case as well as in the other.

Scenario #01: focusing on objectives and disregarding knowledge of customers

The company delivers more or less aggressive content and focuses on the communication of information about its products, rather than offering real solutions.

This type of content does not engage customers, who will either lose all interest in the brand over time or put an end to the link that united them with it.

Scenario #02: focusing on customers and neglecting the definition of objectives

The company offers entertaining content for its customers, who react favorably, but it does not reach any specific objective, because nothing was defined ahead of time.

This type of content does not generate any return on investment. The company certainly advances, but blindly, without any clear direction.

Do not commit the error of producing content left and right, hoping that it will make your audience react. Ensure that by building a strategy which pays off because it is based on tangible proof... and that is certainly what you will do in creating your own strategy based on the roadmap that you are currently discovering!

Creating optimized content means content that:

- takes the expectations of the customers it addresses into consideration;

- respects the codes of each social network;

- belongs to only one particular brand;

- makes the relational tone obvious in customers' eyes.

Provoking the desire of new-generation consumers requires, as mentioned above, seducing them by continuously providing them with solutions. I recommend that you think of content not as content at all, but as solutions. The famous content to be created, which many brand managers dread creating, should in fact be composed of useful and enriching solutions. Solutions that enable customers to make the best consumption choices for themselves and to experience pleasure, strong emotions.

The distinction between the two notions is found at multiple levels:

- Content is generally created at random. Solutions are drawn up in a coherent manner and form a logical progression to reach a precise goal.

– Content provides all kinds of information to a given audience, without specific intent beyond communication about the company's products. Solutions provide, as the name implies, real solutions to customers with which the company communicates.

– Content is generally not drawn up on the basis of a precise knowledge of the customers to be sensitized and mobilized. Solutions respond specifically to the needs and expectations of the target audience.

– Content can be pointless, of no particular interest for customers. Solutions, given that they are intended to respond to the needs and expectations of customers in search of products to consume or feelings to experience, go beyond the surface, to the very heart of the customers' search.

– By publishing content, the company has a discourse and pronounces fine words to vaunt the merits of its products. By sharing solutions, it demonstrates to its customers a real willingness to act in their interest and prove concretely to them that it very probably has the ideal solution that corresponds to what they are looking for.

– Content often gives the impression that the company is trying to impose on its customers what it judges to be best for them. Solutions give them a feeling of freedom of choice, of thriving, and of autonomy.

– Content is ordinarily perishable. Apart from those that are related to short-term actions carried out by the company, solutions are quite imperishable and can be consumed at any moment by Internet users.

Content is published on the pages, accounts and/or channels of a brand to form an ever-growing mass of content. A chain of posts, a succession of campaigns with no real coherence between them. Without order or harmony to guide the customer in his or her search. Actions and posts that have no other purpose beyond being seen. Campaigns made to grab the attention of the target audience and that contribute only to amplifying the ambient noise that reigns on social media. A noise that is more and more disruptive for connected consumers who see a succession of promotional posts when they scroll through their news feeds, bordering on spam.

By focusing on the creation of solutions rather than the production of content, you will take concrete actions, offer precious solutions that will prove to be of priceless value in the eyes of your customers.

Taken collectively, they will represent a coherent whole. They will bring sustainable value, as much to your company as to your customers. Customers who will be motivated to return proactively to your pages, accounts and/or channels in order to inform themselves about what you will have to offer them. Customers in search of what is best for them and what you can offer them.

By guiding your current or potential customers in their search and by proposing solutions without ever imposing anything – giving them, then, the feeling of freedom that they are looking for to make the right choices for themselves, by themselves – you will succeed, over time, in ensuring that the final choice they make falls in your favor. Your offer, represented notably by the entirety of the solutions delivered on a daily basis, will embody THE ideal solution in their eyes, as it corresponds exactly to what they are looking for.

TURN YOUR BUSINESS INTO A RELATIONAL BRAND

BE A PROVIDER OF SOLUTIONS RATHER THAN A SELLER OF PRODUCTS.

Delphine Lang

WWW.DELPHINELANG.COM

As you create your posts, it must become automatic for you to ask the two following questions:

– "Does the article that I am in the process of writing and that I plan to share with connected customers on this or that social network really represent a solution that will help them in their search?"

– "Would I, as a customer of my brand, be truly satisfied to see this article in my news feed, what would push me to make it known by liking it, commenting on it or sharing it within my own network of relationships?"

By being "solutions-oriented", you will see yourself succeed much more quickly at identifying what needs to be done to engage your audience. Consequently, you will feel much more confident in your capacity to create content that your customers will take pleasure in consuming and sharing.

I cannot emphasize this enough: do not limit yourself to what others do. Do not settle for publishing the same content as others while neglecting the demand of your customers, and therefore fail to bring the necessary value-added solutions to fruition. By acting this way, you will risk boxing yourself into a counter-productive and ineffective logic that consists of creating content, posting it and reproducing "what works" at a given moment, without an eye towards the future, for you and your customers.

Remember the essential point: "Do not say things. Act concretely by proving to your customers your capacity to bring them real solutions."

It is quite tempting – and easy – to create a pile of posts with catchy titles to draw attention. Posts that will certainly lead Internet users to react, as they are used to receiving this type of content for consumption.

But if you reproduce what your direct or indirect competitors do, do you sincerely believe that you will succeed in standing out? Very clearly, no. Just because consumers are used to receiving the same content from everywhere does not mean they do not expect something else. And as we have seen before, this is well and truly the case.

It is not a question of creating more content, but of creating content that is useful and enriching and that truly helps your customers in their search for flexible solutions, developed to adapt to their evolving needs and expectations. Solutions that lead your customers to tell themselves that by consuming your products, all of their needs will be met and their expectations will be fully satisfied.

Your solutions must represent sources of value in people's everyday lives. And there are as many ways to create solutions as there are situations where your customers find themselves searching for solutions.

The solutions to be offered to them must be everything they always dreamed of seeing in their news feeds. And you can succeed in this. Be creative in the development of your solutions, staying focused on resolving situations.

Concretely, to create solutions, take one or more situations in which your target consumers find themselves and break down their overall quest into isolated quests to be considered individually.

The ultimate objective is that your offer in its entirety constitutes the ideal solution in the eyes of your customers. The idea is to divide your unique, overall offer into solution units that you will draw up to respond to each isolated quest. The kinds of solutions that, taken collectively, respond effectively to their sophisticated needs (the need for security, the need for belonging, the need for self-esteem and the need for self-actualization) and expectations.

Your customers must be able to find themselves in one single "place" that comprises your pages, your accounts and/or your channels, but also your website or your blog, and find there all the solutions they are looking for. Your solutions must be organized coherently and broadcasted wisely and harmoniously in order to help your customers easily and quickly find everything they need, leading them to say to themselves that they found what they were looking for and to make their choice in your favor.

Always prioritize quality over quantity. Avoid an overload of posts, which is a direct consequence of the traditional process, which consists in creating, posting and reproducing content on a continuous loop. An overabundance of posts could pollute the news feeds of your connected customers rather than enriching them. There is also the risk that your valuable content will be drowned, lost in a plethora of posts, focusing on the communication of information about your products, that are very clearly designed to incite the customer to buy. Your pages and accounts must not look like walls of text, but like a coherent whole that forms a precious resource of solutions.

Generating sales opportunities requires capturing, maintaining and retaining the attention of the members of your online community over time in order to convert them into engaged and loyal customers. Contrary to content, it is what allows an appropriate balance between useful and enriching solutions.

Be sure to alternate between the publication of useful solutions and that of enriching solutions, as well as each type of solution, while maintaining a certain logic in the publication of posts related to an isolated quest. The idea is to aim for a perfect balance between reason and emotions. There is no "rule" at this level, so it is up to you to find yours.

Generally, your solutions must help to facilitate the move from engagement with your brand on social media to the purchase of your products, online or offline. That being said, your customers must get value from your solutions. The latter must "serve" customers efficiently, given that they may not always be purchasing your products, because, as we have seen above, they can also serve as valuable allies by conveying your actions on social media and beyond.

For each solution that you publish, make sure you bring value to your customers by respecting the identity of your brand in order to consolidate a clear position in the minds of your target audience.

By being useful and having value in the eyes of your customers, your solutions will boost the organic – that is to say natural, without having invested in advertising – reach of your posts. They will be therefore more visible in the news feeds of Internet users, which will reduce the necessity of paying more and more for them to be viewed. Appropriate, pertinent solutions being, logically, the most likely to go viral.

Their natural visibility will evolve, certainly less quickly than what is achieved via big-budget ad campaigns, but certainly in the right direction. Stay patient and above all constant in your efforts. In the more or less long term – depending, among other things, on your involvement – you will see that the results speak for themselves. Beneficial results for the growth and development of your activities in the long term.

Keep in mind the following promise: "From the uniqueness of the experience to be lived to the diversity of solutions to be shared." When your posts must be diversified, your intentions, your story, your voice and your visual identity must be unique on all platforms. Nothing should seem like it belongs to a different universe than that of your brand, in order to ensure a marked differentiation between your posts and all of the other posts your customers see in their news feeds.

With the speed at which social network users scroll through posts, a strong identity proves to be essential if you want to succeed in standing out from the crowd. They will then easily be able to associate your content with your brand.

The experience you propose to your customers must above all be designed to convey emotions. In order to ensure this, showcase the visual aspect. Avoid overwhelming your posts with too much text and, as much as possible, insert photos or videos in each of them.

Use words and create images and videos specific to your brand, so your customers will be able to easily make them their own.

Be authentic and adopt the same language codes as those of the people you are addressing. When necessary, create your posts in several versions. We do not talk to a young person the same way we talk to a senior! Their language codes are different and each of the two targeted groups will be motivated to react through posts that are made differently.

If your products are marketed in several countries and if you have a page, an account and/or a channel for each country, it is not enough to translate the content into all of the languages to prove that you are paying attention to your consumers, whichever country they are located in. Adapting content by taking the specificities particular to each country can make all the difference in having an impact with people. This will make them feel that you truly understand them. Consequently, if you manage an international brand add a local touch to heighten awareness even more strongly among your customers.

Step #08: establish an editorial calendar

Once your solutions are created, you must define the frequency of posting and the times (days and hours) at which you will post.

Keep in mind that Internet users remember the frequency of posts of a brand. If they observe that it is not respected, they can very quickly turn away from the brand in question, disappointed that it did not do what was necessary to maintain the relationship with them. It is as though daily newspapers decided not to be available at kiosks on certain days of the week or the weekend because they had nothing to say. Internet users are unforgiving in this regard, so avoid disappointing your public.

Establishing an editorial calendar is relatively simple as long as you know what elements to include, namely: the date, day, time, theme, text content, media (photo or video), url, hashtag, validated (yes/no). All of this must be saved in a document like an Excel® spreadsheet.

Consider your editorial calendar as a bank of solutions in which you will stock the two categories of solutions – beyond the useful and enriching ones – that you will publish on each social network:

- "Timeless" solutions, which can be published at any moment because they have a general character;

- "Time-sensitive" solutions, which you want to share with your audience at a very precise moment.

Make sure you always have enough posts in your bank of solutions. Ideally, for the three upcoming months.

If, on certain days, you do not have a time-sensitive solution to post, you will still have a stock of timeless solutions in reserve. This will allow you to keep the attention of your audience on the days when you have no news in particular and, at the same time, to maintain the link with your customers. You must have understood by now: it's up to you to keep the fire alive!

Step #09: implement a database of customer knowledge

Even though they are still practiced, the traditional segmentations no longer make sense. The consumers of today no longer fit in the boxes where they were previously placed. The customer must, from now on, be considered in relation to several dimensions: time, space and environment.

The same customer is capable of eating in a fast food restaurant for lunch and a five-star restaurant that evening. He or she might be in what we call a white-collar profession and lead a lavish lifestyle, yet prefer to drive a Smart car for the small amount of space it takes up, or even not encumber him- or herself with a car. He or she might have the means to treat himself to a cruise but prefer buying multiple, bargain vacations booked at the last minute on the Internet.

If a customer provides information about him- or herself to a company, he or she expects the company to make good use of it. And especially simply to use it! The trust he or she has in the way in which the data he or she confides is used must be respected.

The digitization of the customer relationship necessarily implies equipment to centralize and organize the collected data on customers. Before investing in CRM (customer relationship management) software[13], identify precisely what you really need in terms of equipment in order to succeed in offering the best possible experience to your customers.

Implement a shared database of customer knowledge across different channels of contact, in which you will centralize data and store all the

---

13. Computer software that facilitates the management of a company's relationship with its customers.

interactions that you will have had with your customers across the various channels. This database will allow you to refine the knowledge you have of your customers and their buying process. You will be subsequently in a position to propose a personalized experience to each one of them, by ensuring the coherence of the delivered content, regardless of the channel chosen by the customer.

Collect all the strategic data on each customer by means of his or her loyalty card, online tracking, as well as, potentially, geo-localization on his or her smartphone, his or her buying process online and in-store, the frequency of his or her visits to your stores, the way in which he or she surfs the Internet, etc. Personalization is ultimately key to attracting more customers, online as well as offline.

By having the history of the interactions you will have had with your customers in your database, you will then have the capacity to model the movements of each customer, Internet and non-Internet user, and make the connections that appear relevant. You will then be capable of offering a personalized experience (personalized promotions, product recommendations, loyalty programs) to each customer and to respond to him or her in an appropriate manner, no matter what channel of contact used. Make use, then, of all the multisource information about the customer by using technologies that aim to make the experience to be lived ultra-personalized and that adapt the relationship to each customer.

It is up to you to ensure excellent customer service, in perfect harmony with what customers expect from you. This necessarily requires adopting a unique vision of the customer, without considering the channel or channels he or she uses to get in touch with you.

Having a customer knowledge database common to the different departments of your company will also allow you to identify or even anticipate certain problems, as well as new opportunities. You will then be in a position to adapt your actions accordingly and to ensure fluidity between the channels at your customers' service – for example, offering the customer the possibility of making his or her purchases online and, if he or she wants to, picking them up at the store.

As much as possible, address each customer personally by adapting your messages and your offers. The idea is to communicate at the right time on the right channels of contact, in order to encourage your customers to react to your messages and consume your products more frequently and lastingly.

Faced with a very heterogeneous market, advanced segmentation is indispensable to anticipate the expectations of your customers and standing out from your competitors.

Segmentation consists in carving out a target group, composed of individuals with diverse and varied characteristics and behaviors, into distinct and homogeneous subgroups. The objective is to address each customer segment in an appropriate manner, by considering the characteristics and behaviors that distinguish the individuals that comprise it from those of other segments.

An efficient and profitable segmentation of a group of consumers to target involves necessarily identifying segmentation criteria linked to characteristics specific to those individuals. Characteristics that explain their consumption habits. There are four principle types of criteria[14].

---

14. Cf. bibliography, n° 5.

Socio-demographic criteria

Because they generate homogenous and accessible segments, these are the most often used criteria.

Types of criteria: gender, age, number of individuals in household, nationality, level of study, salary, height, weight, profession and social class.

Geographic criteria

These have to do with differences relative to lifestyles, climates and traditions.

Types of criteria: place of residence (country, city, urban *vs* rural, etc.), climate (cold, hot or temperate), type of housing (collective *vs* individual, primary residence or secondary residence).

Behavioral criteria

These enable customers to be grouped into homogeneous subgroups from the point of view of their attitudes and behaviors.

Types of criteria: level of consumption (small, medium, or big customer), level of engagement (low-level, mid-level, or very engaged Internet user), buying habits and situations (regular purchases or not, in store or online, personal purchase or gift), advantages that they are looking for (quality, services, etc.), degree of loyalty (regular or occasional customer, non exclusive or not loyal), preferred distribution channel (brand boutiques or large retailers), consumption of media (TV, social media, press, etc.).

Psychographic criteria

These are now quite essential to take into consideration, as the usage of the preceding criteria does not always reveal exploitable segments. Individuals within the same demographic group can have very different psychographic profiles.

Types of criteria: personality (introvert *vs.* extrovert), attitude (active, passive, realistic, skeptical, in search of opinions and advice, etc.), leisure activities, interests (health, fashion, etc.), opinions on particular subjects (openness to the world, belief that we can make the world a better place, etc.).

To achieve an ideal segmentation, the criteria must be chosen as a function of:

– their relevance: the more a criterion used is directly linked to the attitudes and behaviors of customers, the more valuable it is and therefore to be taken into account;

– their measurability: a relevant criterion is one that allows the evaluation of the size of each of the segments for which specific actions will be undertaken;

– their accessibility: the more a criterion enables you to reach accessible segments, the more relevant it is.

As to the implementation, it entails three steps:

1. Identify the usable criteria for the group of consumers to be targeted. Prioritize the distinctive criteria that will allow you to stand out from your competition.

THE QUALITY OF THE CUSTOMER EXPERIENCE IS WHAT CAN MAKE ALL THE DIFFERENCE BETWEEN MAKING THE SALE AND LOSING YOUR CUSTOMERS TO YOUR COMPETITORS.

Delphine Lang

WWW.DELPHINELANG.COM

2. Operate as many simulations as possible with the criteria of segmentation retained in order to identify which ones are really relevant.

3. Keep the criteria that have enabled you to get the best results, while still staying in test and learn mode.

The goal is to end up with a segmentation that is effective and operational.

Finally, know that, in order to enrich your customer knowledge database, there are different possible actions. Do not hesitate to multiply the measures of collecting information and to invite your customers to share their tastes and areas of interest on a personal online space that you will have created especially for them on your website.

With an intelligent management of the data related to your customers, you will be able to identify potential dissatisfaction before your customers express it on social media. From then on, you will be able to predict and anticipate their behaviors, which will unquestionably enable you to increase their satisfaction. With full knowledge of the facts, you will be able to act accordingly.

Step #10: measure your performance and adjust your strategy

For this final step, analyze – with your goals on hand – the effectiveness of your activities, by asking yourself the following questions:

– Were they effective in engaging your customers?

– What were the types of content that worked the best? Which ones did not work as well or did not work at all?

– Have your social media communities grown or stagnated?

Follow the right KPI (key performance indicators) to be aware of the real situation. In part V, you will discover how to usefully and reliably measure your social ROI (return on investment).

On the basis of the collected data, see what lessons can be learned and identify the mistakes that you might have made. It is important to really understand what makes sense to Internet users and, to do this, it is necessary to perform a certain number of trials, or even to make a certain number of errors, in order to understand the subtleties and not to repeat them. Putting yourself in test-and-learn mode is essential for identifying the most effective actions.

Once conclusions have been drawn, adjust your strategy accordingly in order to achieve better results. If one type of solution worked particularly well, it is wise to reprogram it into your editorial calendar. Conversely, a type of solution that has triggered little reaction from Internet users will likely no longer have a place among your upcoming posts.

Getting closer to your customers by taking full advantage of all of the opportunities offered by social media in terms of dialogue, exchange and sharing will allow you to collect suggestions for improvement and to always have a better grasp of their needs and expectations. Every great accomplishment requires time. Be patient and take the time necessary to build your own strategy on the basis of the SocialKind approach that you have just discovered. A strategy that will be yours, unique, and will allow you to stand out from your competitors. A clear and coherent strategy that will enable you to build, maintain and strengthen trust-based relationships with your customers. This is the guarantee of lasting and rewarding success for all.

One last essential point: make the contribution of your activities to the growth and success of your company as a whole known among all your collaborators. Good knowledge of the results by all staff members will ensure their engagement in the actions carried out on social media platforms.

3. How to act: adopt the 12 fundamental best practices

Within the context of implementing your strategy, it will be indispensable for you to follow a series of fundamental practices to ensure your success.

Here are the twelve fundamental practices to adopt.

Practice #01: use the codes specific to social media

It is indispensable that you master the codes specific to social media in order to demonstrate your professionalism, but especially to be effective in your communication and to waste as little time as possible in the creation of your posts.

Certain codes are common to all platforms, whereas others are specific to one or several of them.

For example, use smileys on the different platforms to create empathy, or hashtags so that Internet users who may be interested in your products can find your posts when they do research on Instagram or Twitter. On Twitter in particular, familiarize yourself with the simplified writing style used for the drafting of tweets, the common abbreviations such as DM (direct message) or IMHO (in my humble opinion)... And many other codes you must absolutely be familiar with and that you can easily find out through Internet search engines.

Practice #02: publish regularly and at the right time

It is essential to know the best times of the day to post your content. This question is all the more relevant when we know that timing may single-handedly determine the impact your posts have. Imagine that you publish an article or a video on your Facebook page or on your YouTube channel, but it goes unnoticed simply because your audience is asleep at the time you post... All that effort to end up being seen by nobody. It is thus imperative that you avoid getting trapped in this annoying situation by knowing the right times to post.

Social media users want companies to regularly provide them with rich content about their favorite brands. They only proactively go back to the Facebook page or Instagram account of a brand when the latter has proven to them that they can count on it to be told new stories on a daily basis.

The very nature of platforms is constantly changing and the organic reach of published content decreasing on each of them. This explains the importance of maintaining regular frequency in your posts.

The explanation of the importance of publishing as regularly as possible – the ideal being a minimum of one post per day – is explained in the algorithm of a platform such as Facebook. An algorithm that governs the publication of posts in the news feeds of its users on the basis of certain rules. Rules specific to each platform. On Facebook, priority is given to content published by the "strongest" companies, meaning the ones which amplify and/or have understood the rules of the game, to the detriment of the "weakest" companies, meaning the ones that do not amplify and/or are present without knowing the rules of the game.

The Facebook algorithm is composed of three variables:

- Affinity: the more a fan of your page reacts to your posts, the more your content will be visible in his or her news feed. If his or her engagement decreases – and therefore he or she is less interested in what you publish – the visibility of your posts in his or her news feed will also decrease;

- Frequency: a recent post will have a better chance of being placed at the top of the ranking and therefore of being visible in your fans' news feed;

- Weight: integrating photos, videos, status updates, offers and links in your posts will encourage their visibility as well as the number of reactions (likes, comments, shares, clicks on links, etc.), generated by each of them.

In order to increase the organic reach of your posts, you must thus strive to maintain the affinity between your brand and your fans, post regularly, integrate the "right" elements and publish content that will make them react.

A news feed has limited space. A limited space for more and more competitors entering the race. And therefore a constant increase in the number of posts disseminated every day on the platform. Facebook is therefore obliged to implement more "drastic" rules and give a more prominent place to those who pay for ad campaigns that appear in the news feed of its users. Regardless of whether or not we think this is fair, it is quite logical.

However, contrary to the commonly held notion that the organic reach of posts is definitively dead, forcing companies to pay to be seen, many ways still exist to raise it. Instead of focusing on amplifying the visibility of your content by investing in ad campaigns, concentrate primarily on creating content that will be searched for by your customers, which will motivate them to engage and proactively go to your Facebook page, your Twitter or Instagram account, etc. It goes without saying that ad campaigns will be necessary and indispensable, but invest in campaigns to boost the visibility of content you will have created with the assurance that it will interest and appeal to your audience, and that the latter will react in large numbers.

Sustained activity combined with high value-added content is certain to boost the organic reach of your posts. Consistency in your efforts, without ever letting your guard down, will produce visible results in the long term.

By maintaining daily contact with your audience, you will acquire a better knowledge of your customers and you will thus be prepared to serve them better. You will then be able to strengthen your skills, acquire new skills and, from then on, continuously improve your offer so that it corresponds specifically to what your customers expect from you.

Practice #03: ensure constant monitoring

Every brand wants to portray a positive image of itself and its products, one that is intended to be powerfully anchored in the minds of its customers. The challenge is standing out. To distinguish oneself from the competition.

While it is pleasant and easy to receive compliments, you probably know the old saying about how bad news always seems to travel faster than good news. The more your brand is recognized, the more you expose yourself to the dissatisfaction of your customers (because they are much more numerous).

It is sometimes difficult to control the entire commercial chain and when a link breaks, brand managers find themselves front and center with dissatisfied customers.

These days, consumers wield unprecedented power over a brand's reputation. If a customer has a negative experience with a brand, he or she will seek to harm it by writing a message directly to the brand or by relaying negative information expressed by other Internet users. If the company, by way of its brand managers, does not react immediately, it increases the risk of bad buzz. A phenomenon that can seriously damage its image. The slightest failure can have dramatic consequences and transform a simple point of contention, which would have been trivial in the past, into large-scale crisis management.

Ensuring constant monitoring of what Internet users are saying about your brand is therefore indispensable to managing your online reputation effectively. Identify all your customers' reactions, the discussions that come with them, and those participating in them, in order to be prepared to respond to a conflict immediately, before things go wrong.

Being watchful is an ideal way to prove to your customers that you are attentive to their problems or criticisms and that you take all these into account in order to improve what must be improved. Active involvement is the antidote to mistrust and gratuitous criticism, especially when the sector makes this easy (telephony, for example). If Internet users know you are there to reply to customer reactions, it is clear that they will think twice before unleashing negative comments...

It is clearly important to implement sufficient resources in order to ensure that platforms through which customers can contact you are perfectly operational. A sufficient number of people, consistent monitoring and qualified staff, connected to the company's other departments, are required. In certain cases, weekend support staff may be needed (telephone operators are a perfect example).

This sufficient allocation of resources and professionalization of staff are both essential to managing and ensuring a quick and effective response to all your customers' requests.

Practice #04: deal with all requests

Any mention of your brand – in particular, complaints, requests for information and suggestions – on the different places of discussion, must be taken into consideration, which necessitates permanent monitoring of your products, your brand and your company.

Customers no longer limit sharing information about the problems they encounter on your Facebook page, your Twitter account or your blog. They also do so in forums, on their own blog, on consumer review websites, etc.

For example, thanks to hashtags on social networking sites, you can stay informed in real time about what is being said, good or bad, about you and your brand, which means you will be able to react immediately. Make sure you activate push notifications on your smartphone to see reactions from Internet users the moment they share them on the various platforms.

It is important to determine the degrees of priority and urgency of customer requests and then rank them and deal with the priority requests before the rest. Some of them are of secondary importance – which of course shouldn't stop you from answering them – whereas others are a priority and require a quick or even immediate response. For instance, the request from a customer dissatisfied with a defective product or a call center that is not answering comes before dealing with a request for general information or a suggestion.

In all situations, you must demonstrate to each customer that he or she is important to you by taking great care to answer all requests.

Practice #05: listen attentively and empathetically

To respond to complaints posted on social networking sites, the need to show understanding is indispensable. Have you never experienced the frustration of receiving the wrong item or one that is faulty? Have you never stormed out of a store where you were treated poorly? Remember such situations and imagine how you would have wanted to be treated when explaining your grievance. Most certainly with empathy, sympathy and efficiency. Well then, treat your customers the way you would like to be treated. Even if it is often not the case, the customer always believes that his or her problem is unique and expects the brand managers with whom he or she speaks with on social media to show they are really listening.

To reply to a customer appropriately, it is crucial to accurately understand the nature of his or her request, which can only happen if you "listen[15]" to him or her attentively and empathetically. Give the customer time to explain his or her problem. Even if you have dealt with the problem mentioned time and time again, the customer must get the impression that you are fully attentive. Thus avoid reacting instantaneously with a standard answer that could give the customer the annoying and disagreeable impression of being nothing more than a number.

---

15. Even if you are in this case interacting with your customers through social media, the fact that you are listening must be felt in the answers you provide them.

Listen to everything he or she has to tell you. Once he or she has explained everything and you have understood the problem well, you will be ready to reply, but not before. There are two possible situations: either the problem can be resolved immediately or you will need to get more information before providing him or her with a solution. In this case, inform the customer of how you will solve the problem and how quickly you will get back to him or her. Make your customer understand that you are on his or her side and that you would probably react in a similar manner if you were in the same situation, by using expressions like "I understand" or "Thank you for having alerted us to this fault".

If you cannot do anything, tell your customer. It is not always possible to find a solution to every problem encountered by your customers, though this should not by any means make you deaf to their concerns. Do not delete negative comments... with the exception of gratuitous criticism and baseless attacks.

Demonstrate attentive listening and empathy. Your connected customers will undoubtedly take notice, which will reinforce their trust in both your brand and your company.

Practice #06: respond quickly

Customers want to be able to reach someone at any time, no matter where they are, and to get a quick reply through the contact channel of their choosing to get their problems solved.

These days, customers are turning more and more to social media to contact brand managers and express their problems or ask them for additional information before or after purchase. Nothing is simpler than commenting on a post, or sending a message through the Facebook page or posting a tweet on the Twitter account of a brand. It is a way to save both time and energy, quite the opposite of the interminable waits when calling customer service or sending an email and not knowing if anyone will read it.

Given the expectations of connected consumers, you must demonstrate your ability to respect the notion of instantaneousness inherent to social media and be as responsive as possible. It is your responsibility to react quickly to every request you receive from your customers in order to prove to them that they can count on you to get a response through social media as quickly as, or even quicker than by phone or by email. This implies ensuring a presence on the days and at the times your consumers are connected – including weekends.

You should also avoid the snowball effect that results when a customer problem has not been handled, encouraging other customers to react negatively. Do not leave the door open to disgruntled customers who are looking for an opportunity to publicly share their unexpressed discontent.

If it is impossible to meet all your customer requests in the time frames they hope for, it is your responsibility to demonstrate to your customers that you have taken their questions into account and that you will do your best to satisfy them. This will prevent them from losing patience and expressing their discontent in the event you do not react.

Do your utmost to reply to each request from a current or potential customer within twenty-four hours, on the same channel as the one he or she contacted you on, whether it be to inform him or her that you have found a solution to his or her problem, or to confirm you have taken his or her request into consideration and that you will get back to him or her as soon as possible with a solution to the problem. A simple action, such as an appropriate response in due time – even if it is not the expected solution – may sometimes make all the difference in the eyes of your customers.

Do not, however, feel obliged to give a solution immediately. You may need to do some research or make some phone calls to get a precise answer (for example, contacting your in-store sales people). Ensure that you bring a final answer to each individual who has sent you a request and to whom you have given a first response, whether or not you was able to solve his or her problem.

Make sure you are responsive but do not make any false promises binding you to time frames you will not be able to keep, such as, for example, a reply within an hour which you would be unable to do for whatever reason. This could potentially increase the frustration and dissatisfaction of customers, which must be avoided at all costs.

If you have a Twitter account dedicated to customer service, think of indicating to Internet users the hours when you are absent or unavailable, so that they know that their request will not be seen immediately, and at what time you will be again reachable and available. Specify the duration of your absence or unavailability through a message such as "See you tomorrow at 8 am. Have a good evening everyone!" The same goes for informing Internet users of your presence in the morning and the time when you are again reachable, wishing them "Good morning!"

Do not employ technical terms that only you understand, which only confuses customers and leads them to question the effectiveness of your customer service.

Reflect an image of a company that is human-oriented and close to its customers by signing your replies to your connected customers' requests.

---

18. Bien que vous soyez en l'occurrence en interaction avec vos clients via les réseaux sociaux, l'écoute doit se ressentir dans les réponses que vous leur donnez.

Customer follow-up will then be even more personalized, which will contribute to increasing the level of customer satisfaction. This also has a reassuring aspect for the customer, who, whether he or she has been in contact with your customer service or not, will say to himself or herself that there are real "human beings" behind the brand with whom he or she is connected through social media. Individuals with whom he or she will speak directly the day when he or she may need to contact them (again). Emphasizing in this way customer service managers within your company will unquestionably help reinforce the trust your customers have in your brand more strongly.

Practice #07: participate in discussions

Always keep in mind that the customer relationship works in two directions. If consumers share their opinions with you about your brand and your products, they expect you to be equally engaged, notably by participating in discussions.

Managing a customer relationship on social media is a way of engagement with, on the consumer side, requirements in terms of responsiveness, flexibility in the discussions, solutions offered... Too many companies act as if social media were "free" billboards, limiting themselves to promoting their products and neglecting or completely ignoring the relational aspect. There is a fine line between self-promotion and spamming, and customers will very quickly turn away from you if they see that you are not involved. More than just a discourse, establish two-way communication. In order to get your customers involved, always keep in mind that you need to be involved as well. When they need to purchase the products you are selling, they will be more likely to turn to you, especially if you have already proven to them your responsiveness and effectiveness.

TURN YOUR BUSINESS INTO A RELATIONAL BRAND

GIVE YOUR CONNECTED CUSTOMERS THE OPPORTUNITY TO FEEL VALUED, INVOLVED AND HEARD, JUST BECAUSE THEY'RE PEOPLE LIKE YOU AND ME.

Delphine Lang

WWW.DELPHINELANG.COM

With regard to the customer who has not yet consumed your products, he or she will be reassured to know that if a problem arises after purchase, you will be there to deal with and resolve it.

The engagement you will demonstrate on social media will unquestionably help your customers, current or potential, feel reassured, which is indispensable to building their trust in your brand.

Practice #08: provide guidance and direction

Not all problems can be solved through social media. If consumers are accustomed to contacting the customer service of a company by phone, customer requests received by it will likely need to be dealt with outside of social media.

If this is the case for you, clearly indicate to your customers the process to follow to move their request forward and guide them towards the appropriate contact channels so that they can get the information they are looking for.

As much as possible, avoid abruptly transferring the customer request to different contact channels. If you cannot do otherwise, make sure the information about the problem for which he or she has contacted you through social media is transferred to the collaborators in your other departments in order to avoid the customer having to explain the problem again. This would only increase his or her dissatisfaction and drive him or her to express it on the web.

Furthermore, do not commit the error of proposing features reserved exclusively for customers and to which prospective customers do not have access. This may generate a feeling of frustration and exclusion, which will extinguish their desire from the outset to find out more about your brand and buy your products. Each prospect is a potential future customer. It is therefore in your best interest to conquer and convince your potential buyers by helping them in their search for information.

Practice #09: demonstrate transparency and sincerity

Before the emergence of social media, companies had the habit of covering up their errors and only communicating "the positive". The goal was to preserve a perfect, apparently solid image.

It is now high time to stop behaving this way. Consumers do not prefer so-called perfect brands in which they cannot recognize themselves. They are searching for authentic brands that have human values and demonstrate transparency and sincerity.

Thanks to the plethora of information sources to which they have access, consumers today can very quickly and easily see through brands that proclaim that they are perfect – as well as false promises. If defects for which you would be responsible arise, do not try to hide them. To err is human... and the mistakes you may have made will be forgiven more easily if you recognize them and apologize for them straightaway instead of making efforts to hide them.

When dissatisfaction is justified and there really was a mistake on your part, it is essential to take whatever action necessary to correct the error in order to resolve any complaint as quickly and as effectively as possible.

The important thing is to show the customer that you acknowledge your mistake and that you will do your utmost to both remedy the situation in the shortest possible time and to find a solution.

Acknowledging your mistakes and taking responsibility for them is a major guarantee of quality. It is a credit to you to admit a mistake and can resolve a contentious dialogue. Beyond that, it is the best way to build a community of satisfied, engaged and loyal customers and to convince others to be part of it.

If it proves to be necessary, offer your apologies to your customers. "We are sincerely sorry" are words that can have a soothing effect on an angry Internet user and calm his or her discontent. Starting your message in reply to a customer complaint in this way helps start a peaceful conversation which will lead to a smooth resolution of the crisis. Apologies are generally received very well by dissatisfied customers. Sincere apologies followed by compensation should help you get back into the good graces of the consumer and ultimately turn his or her dissatisfaction into satisfaction.

Remember that the customer is always right. If this is not the case and the problem, entirely or in part, does not come from you, it is up to you to prove the contrary and to support your answers by facts and evidence. Avoid blaming others in your response. Acting in such a way will certainly not solve the problem, and the customer – or someone else – will come back even more dissatisfied than he was before. Simply answer him or her by including any third parties concerned in your answer. Otherwise judiciously make him or her understand that he or she was perhaps responsible.

Practice #10: calm things down and use private messages

It is well known that one does not wash one's dirty laundry in public. The same applies for resolving problems that can sometimes drag out or that simply require sending private information such as a credit card number or an address.

In such situations, suggest that your customer sends you the required information in a private message. This is a much more appropriate way to discuss and resolve possible conflicts.

Private messaging also helps to avoid negative comments from a dissatisfied customer going public and "tarnishing" your pages, your accounts and/or your channels, which can have an extremely negative impact on the opinion other consumers form of you and your products.

When confronted with an aggressive customer, a demanding customer or a chronic complainer, it is always preferable to keep the conversation private in order to mitigate the impact of his or her uncontrollable reactions.

The procedure to follow is simple and must become systematic for all requests that necessitate shifting to private mode: publicly reply to the customer stating that you have indeed acknowledged his or her request and that you will resolve the issue directly with him or her by private message.

Be courteous and polite in all circumstances. When confronted with a customer who is stubborn and annoyed, remain calm. It seems that is easier to say this than to do it. Nevertheless, always keep in mind that your reputation is at stake.

If you receive a particularly vicious message from an aggressive customer, do not react on your emotions and do not take criticism personally. Take time to formulate your response. By responding awkwardly, you risk alienating other consumers who can see your reactions.

Think of including signs of respect and consideration for your customers, whether in your posts or in private messages, in order to avoid bad buzz resulting from the poor handling of a customer problem.

If you do everything in your power to respond in the best possible way to a customer and yet he or she continues to complain, it may be that no matter what you do, he or she will remain dissatisfied. In this case, you are very likely dealing with a "troll"...

Trolls are Internet users who like to sully social networks, blogs and forums with negative comments, which are very often totally baseless. They make vicious comments or even gratuitous attacks. These are not necessarily consumers of your products. They may never have actually purchased anything from you, but they will ceaselessly criticize you by commenting on your posts.

If you are dealing with such individuals, do not get involved in their game by starting a battle of arguments. This may take a long time and in any case you will never be right! All that they want is to attack you and to see how you will react, hoping that you will get carried away. The solution: simply block them. If you can muster it, you can try using humor to show that they have been unmasked, but it is essential to stop after one interaction. Think of the expression "Don't feed the troll". Nothing will stop them, except ignoring them.

Practice #11: solicit influencers

What sells today is not advertising but word of mouth through recommendations and testimonials from "brand ambassadors" and "influencers". Given the confusion very often made between these two terms, it is important to clarify what each means and how they are different.

Brand ambassadors are customers who are highly engaged on social networking sites, who trust a brand because they were come fully satisfied from the experience proposed by the brand while having generally consumed its products, and make it known by promoting it on the web, and this without any compensation. These are largely customers who have major power of influence over the consumption choices of other Internet users. Indeed, some customers of a brand may be very active on social media platforms but not at all influential over other consumers simply because they do not have a wide enough audience. They may be as engaged as possible, but they influence no one or a very few people, which means their engagement, even if positive, will have little value in significantly growing the visibility of the brand on social media. It is therefore indispensable that the customers considered as "brand ambassadors" do in fact wield considerable power of influence on the Internet in order to be considered as such.

Influencers (bloggers, celebrities, experts) are generally recognized and respected figures in their field of activity who have a large following on social media. Few in number and highly sought after, their interest in collaborating with a brand is first and foremost commercial: they will promote a brand if they receive remuneration or other advantage in exchange (free products, invitations to private sales, etc.) for their involvement in extolling its merits.

What fundamentally differentiates the two is mainly brand loyalty. Influencers are fickle, whereas brand ambassadors are extremely loyal, which means the latter are more likely to serve the interests of a brand over the long term.

In the eyes of their peers, recommendations and testimonials from brand ambassadors are considered more credible and reliable than those from influencers. Therefore, based on their own experience with the brand and their willingness to help consumers make the best choice for themselves, brand ambassadors are more likely to influence the buying behaviors of other consumers.

There are multiple motivating factors that drive influencers active on social media platforms to promote a brand to accept a collaboration: high visibility generated by the activities carried out by the brand, quality content to share with their public, a beneficial impact on their own image, etc. These days, the influencer phenomenon has taken on such a scale that consumers are no longer fooled and can quickly detect those whose aims are strictly financial and do not serve the interests of their audience. They are completely aware that the influencers they follow on social media and to whom they turn for reliable tips before purchasing are very often paid or receive the products they promote for free. They therefore quickly and easily decode all the techniques used to get them to buy.

In any event, the promotion of a brand is particularly effective when it is done by those who are truly passionate about the brand. Therefore, in my opinion, such people may be both brand ambassadors and influencers if they perfectly embody the spirit of the brand and are aligned with its values.

By their strong and continuous involvement and their high level of activity, certain brand ambassadors can see their audience grow in a very short amount of time, and thus be sought after by brands in exchange for compensation and thereby become true influencers, which means that there is a fine line between the two terms. This is the reason why I recommend you call on "influencers", whether they are well-known influencers or brand ambassadors who have a significant power to influence other consumers through social media (social networks, blogs, forums, etc.).

The idea is to combine the two effectively, knowing that calling on influencers represents a certain cost. In any case, calling on either the one and/or the other to promote your brand – after making a judicious selection – you will have a much greater chance of getting your products adopted than through a classic ad campaign. The engagement level of the consumers you want to seduce and convince will often be much higher if you involve influencers, therefore allowing you to significantly increase your return on investment.

However, keep in mind that influencers cannot always be molded, and the individual who makes a wrong step may have a negative influence on the brand image. Those who are constantly seeking to get more and more – whether of fans and followers or money and free products – exploit this type of operation, ending up losing all their credibility among the members of their online community. Use these techniques to promote your brand and your products on social media, but do not abuse them!

A brief aside: in the final part of this book, you will discover how to set up effective and profitable collaborations with influencers.

Practice #12: reward loyalty at two levels

When customers engage with a brand, either by buying its products or sharing its messages on social media, they expect the company to reward their loyalty.

Measures rewarding the loyalty of one's engaged customers, such as discounts and other promotional incentives, are essential for retaining them and motivating them to continue acting in this way. These practices should encourage multiple purchases and should instantly recognize customer loyalty, unlike the approach that aims to thank the customer after a certain period of time.

If you want to delight them, make sure you recognize their loyalty throughout the entire customer journey rather than simply at the time of purchase. In other words, recognize your customers as much for their purchase of your products as for their engagement with your posts. Acting in this way can only lead to one attitude among your customers: more engagement and remaining unquestionably more loyal to your brand. For a long time.

TURN YOUR BUSINESS INTO A RELATIONAL BRAND

DON'T BE KNOWN FOR WHAT YOU SAY TO SELL YOUR PRODUCTS. BE RECOGNIZED FOR WHAT YOU DO TO ENRICH PEOPLE'S LIVES.

Delphine Lang

WWW.DELPHINELANG.COM

Results

The success of your social media activities depends on the acquisition of knowledge and skills essential to provide your customers with an offer that fulfills their expectations and requirements.

Once this is achieved, you will succeed, with the adoption of the SocialKind approach, in proving to your customers that you are on social media platforms not because you have to be, but because you are motivated by a real desire to help them make the best decisions for themselves. An unrivalled guarantee of trust that will encourage them to call on you rather than others. This will enable you to stand out from the competition and give you an intangible competitive advantage, difficult to emulate.

I. Maximize your impact, your power of influence and your performance

By drawing up and implementing an innovative growth strategy for your brand, you will succeed in building, maintaining and strengthening trust-based relationships with your customers. By sharing, each day, useful and enriching solutions with your customers, in search of what is best for them and what you offer them, you will amplify your impact and significantly reinforce your power of influence. You will then occupy a prominent place in their hearts and in their minds. Customers who will willingly go onto your Facebook page, your Twitter and/or Instagram account, your YouTube channel, etc., but also into your stores, as soon as they feel the need.

By succeeding in making the relationship with your brand obvious in the eyes of consumers, through the immersion into a unique and precious experience that corresponds very precisely to their expectations and satisfies every last desire, you will succeed, over time, in positioning yourself as an essential partner for your customers and being a part of their daily life.

You will increase their level of loyalty to your brand and, consequently, their level of consumption of your messages and products.

Effective and coherent management of your social media presence will translate into positive recommendations and testimonials from customers who are satisfied with the experience they have had with your brand and your products, which represents the best guarantee to ensure your growth and development on social media.

II. Measure your social ROI with relevance and reliability

Being able to effectively measure the performance of one's social media activities is of major interest for any company. However, there is an important – and worrying – gap between companies that expand into social media platforms and their capacity to effectively measure their return on their investments.

Although measuring ROI is not simple, it is not optional. As with any other channel of communication, measurement is an essential component in the success of one's activities. Indispensable for making strategic decisions and budgetary choices by managers, who are logically more likely to invest in media for which the ROI is guaranteed because it is accurately measured, effective measurement of one's return on investment on social media enables one to evaluate the human and financial resources to allocate, estimate the time to spend and determine the most appropriate channels for achieving the desired results.

For executive management, many of whom may still be reticent because they have preconceived ideas or because they lack understanding, tangible evidence should be given, enabling the justification of deployment on social media platforms, in order to convince them of their usefulness and to encourage them to call on the engagement of all of their collaborators in their social media activities.

For those who manage the social presence of a brand on a daily basis – whether their own, that of the company that employs them or that they collaborate with (in the case of an agency) – the majority of whom feel that their efforts pay off even if they measure their performance a little or not at all, the importance of measuring is to ensure that what they do is truly effective and, in such a case, to recognize the efforts invested. In the opposite case, while providing evidence, the aim is to avoid continuing to undertake efforts that cannot meet the objectives set, by taking appropriate measures in order to reinforce their effectiveness.

A. Current measuring practices

On traditional channels of communication like television and radio, companies evaluate the impact of their campaigns at different points on the customer journey. On social media, the journey followed by the customer is different. However, the measurement practices remain unchanged. Companies evaluate customer value by using a combination of metrics[16] – number of fans, number of interactions (likes, comments, shares), engagement rate, etc. – provided by the platforms themselves or other specific measurement tools widely available on the market. They therefore report the performance of their campaigns on the basis of traditional KPIs.

---

16. Another term to refer to measurement indicators.

These sources deliver data measuring the rate of success at each step of the customer journey. To illustrate:

- Attention: the number of views gives an idea of the increase in brand visibility.

- Interest: the number of fans reflects consumer interest in the products.

- Desire: the engagement rate indicates purchase intention.

- Action: online purchases reflect the rate of conversion of consumers into buyers.

The evaluation of customer value is based therefore on the amount that he or she will spend on the brand's products over the course of his or her life.

B. Why change

These data only show one static image of the performance of a company's social media activities. Taken together, they represent only one aspect of their effectiveness. They do not reveal any of their true added value, that is to say, to what extent they have actually been really effective at contributing to the growth and development of the company as a whole.

One is very clearly focusing on quantity and neglecting quality.

Not knowing if what they do is effective or not, brand managers are incapable of making reasoned decisions to ensure the prosperity of their company.

Even high achievement levels do not in any way guarantee the success of one's social media activities. Here are five ways to justify such an assertion.

Fact #1: likes and follows do not last forever

Likes and follows[17] do not have a clear and universal meaning, without even taking into account the fact that they are not everlasting. For some social media users, liking a page is a way of saying that they truly like the brand. For others, it simply means that they are authorizing the brand to contact them, more often for a specified period of time – for example, for the duration of a campaign, because the brand has required them to like its page in order to participate in a competition.

In any case, people who like pages expect something in return from the brands they are connected to: discount vouchers and promotions that they might use at the time of purchase, exclusive offers that they cannot find anywhere else and invitations to events, but, above all, interactions with the brand and with other members of the community gathered around it.

They actively manage their connections with brands, purely and simply deleting those they no longer find useful and/or those who have not done anything to demonstrate reciprocal engagement. The reasons for an "unlike" are many: loss of relevance in relation to one's lifestyle, desire to change brands or a contest which has finished.

To return to the current measurement, if a brand manager does not know what was effective in terms of actions, he or she cannot adapt his or her strategy in order to publish content that customers will like and consume. As a result, the risk of losing them is much higher.

---

17. Follows of an account by Internet users on platforms like Twitter and Instagram.

Fact #02: high values, yes, but ad campaigns

Clearly demonstrating their short-term vision, the majority of companies present on social media platforms produce content that they amplify with ad campaigns.

No matter what the type of campaign, they are guaranteed an increase in their number of fans or reactions with a guaranteed rate of success. In the short term, they get what they were promised. They are presented with graphics and dashboards where their performance is compared to that of their competitors, with metrics of a purely quantitative aspect that illustrate the so-called success of the campaign. Spectacular but meaningless data.

Indeed, quantity does not make quality. In the short term, the quantity index is positive. The company has grown in quantity, because the traditional metrics are there to prove it. What is nevertheless not assured is the quality index. And there, nothing and no one can guarantee that it has grown in quality, because there is no metric to demonstrate it.

The growth in number of fans taken in isolation does not mean that success is around the corner. Indeed, if the number of fans increases exponentially during a campaign, but the average level of engagement decreases proportionally, the organic reach – already very weak – of the posts of a brand will fall drastically. In the following months, the company will have to redouble its efforts to conserve or win back its audience's attention to its brand.

All of this, without even taking into account the fact that many of hard-won fans are often fake fans, without any value for the company. Fake accounts or people who are paid to like pages, but who will never set foot in a store.

RATHER THAN STRIVING TO BE BETTER THAN YOUR COMPETITORS, STRIVE TO BE THE BEST FOR YOUR CUSTOMERS.

Delphine Lang

WWW.DELPHINELANG.COM

Fact #3: high values but many fans and/or posts

The various metrics commonly used are influenced by two variables:

- Fans: the larger a brand's community on social media is, the higher the probability that the number of actions generated on its posts is as well.

- Posts: the greater the quantity of posts of a brand during a given period of time, the higher the probability that the number of actions generated on its posts as a whole is high as well.

Having a greater number of reactions than one's competitors does not therefore mean that one is necessarily performing better, and vice versa. Consequently, making decisions on the basis of a comparison of performance with other market players active on social media platforms is nonsense.

The potential for growth is much higher with a few members who are strongly engaged than with an army of inactive fans, who will probably not be motivated to follow you eternally and will therefore have little value.

Fact #4: a high engagement rate is not always positive

If you compare your performance to that of your competitors on the basis of engagement rate, you may arrive at the conclusion that you have been less successful at engaging your connected customers – who might be the same individuals in the case of direct competitors are concerned. Yet, during bad buzz, a brand's posts can generate a great many reactions, and therefore strong engagement.

This high engagement rate does not signify success since the large-scale reaction will negatively impact the image of the brand concerned.

Fact #5: high values, not always synonymous with sales

The most engaged fans of your online community are not always the biggest buyers. However, they can bring you a large number of new customers and are therefore of great value – which does not combine well with a short-term vision, because the transformation of individuals into strongly engaged fans takes time.

In conclusion, the data that are currently used by companies to measure their social ROI do not give any indication of "what really counts", that is to say what allows one to guarantee a positive ROI. This incorrect interpretation of the relative performance of different actors in a given sector of activity can only lead to error in the actions to be undertaken that come from such a comparative analysis. Consequently, it does not enable one to make sound decisions nor to act effectively in order to adjust one's strategy accordingly.

The current measurement process further slows companies' understanding of how to use social use to ensure the growth and success of their businesses.

Traditional metrics do not give any fair or reliable indication of the success of a brand on social media. These performance indicators are, however, the most commonly used.

The popularity of current measures can be explained by various reasons:

– They are simple, since they are numbers.

– They are consistent with the measurement practices in traditional media.

– They are clear and easily communicable to management.

Without any guarantee of the effectiveness of one's social media activities, it is high time to stop hindering oneself with a plethora of data that only gives the impression of drowning, and above all of understanding and controlling nothing. Instead, it is a question of concentrating on what is essential. On what really counts.

Worry less about what the others – direct or indirect competitors – are doing, and be more concerned about what the consumers that you are aiming to seduce and convince expect from companies like yours on social media. In other words, do not focus all of your attention on classic metrics, but go further and obtain reliable lessons by giving meaning to the data.

C. The SocialKind philosophy on the social ROI measurement

As we have seen, in the digital world today, limiting oneself to simply satisfying one's customers through the communication of information about one's products is no longer enough. To guarantee their engagement, you must make them feel understood, valued and recognized for what they are – simply because they are people like you and me – by using technology intelligently and effectively in order to provide them with an offer that fulfills or even anticipates their every last desire.

On the basis of the SocialKind approach, the goal to set oneself is to turn one's business into a relational brand by building, maintaining and strengthening trust-based relationships with one's customers over time.

The attitude to adopt is the following: stop blindly investing in ad campaigns without any guarantee of significant long-term results, but rather concentrate on what really counts to ensure a return on one's investments, therefore guaranteeing continual growth and the success of one's company.

Different from other channels of communication, the nature inherent to social media consists in developing a customer relationship made of recurring events that have an influence on the value of the brand. Something that develops with time, hence the necessity of adopting a long-term vision.

What is truly important and what one neglects in the majority of current measures:

- IS NOT the position of a brand in a competitive environment at a given moment, but IS the relationship it develops with its customers over time;

- IS NOT the quantity, that is to say the number of fans or reactions, which does not give any competitive advantage in the long term, but IS the quality, that is to say the trust customers have for a brand, which enables it to attract them, to convince them and to retain them;

- IS NOT conversion, that is to say striving exclusively to convert one's fans into buyers, but IS the conversation, by striving to convert one's fans, if not into buyers, then into brand ambassadors.

You must worry less about what others – your direct or indirect competitors – do and instead be more concerned about what the consumers that you seek to attract and convert into loyal and engaged customers expect from companies like yours on social media. In other words, not focusing all of your attention on classic metrics, but going beyond mere quantitative logic and finding reliable information, by giving meaning to figures.

The best indication of the success of a company on social media is not the value it has created today, over the course of a campaign, but rather its ability to create value today and tomorrow.

By drawing up and implementing your own strategy on the basis of the SocialKind approach, you will succeed in building, maintaining and strengthening trust-based relationships with your customers. It is therefore for you the absolute guarantee of maximizing your return on investment by creating long-term value for all of the actors involved: your company, your investors, your customers and society at large.

III. Leverage trust-based relationships with your influencers

Once you will have succeeded, with time, in gaining the trust of your customers, you will have a certain number of customers who will have trust in your brand and who have the power to influence others. This core, more or less large, of influencers – as a reminder, either famous influencers or brand ambassadors – represents the best way to promote your brand and significantly increase the visibility of your brand and your actions on social media platforms. It is therefore a matter of leveraging these trust-based relationships by establishing fruitful collaborations with them. With their power of influence, their attentive and loyal community, they represent a real opportunity to boost your reputation and your brand's image, so make the most of it!

Today more than ever, influencers are at the core of actions led by many brands on social media, and this in multiple fields. Many of them set up special operations by inviting influencers like bloggers to exclusively discover their new products before their release on the market. The result of such operations: a shower of praise on the web in the hours that follow. Do not miss out on such an opportunity, knowing that you will have given the best of yourself to provide your customers – among which there are undeniably some influencers – a valuable experience that will have enabled you to gain their trust.

To establish effective collaborations with influencers, there is a five-step procedure to follow.

Step #01: precisely set your objectives

Objectives can be numerous: establish one's reputation, reinforce the quality image of one's brand, increase the online visibility of one's brand and actions, promote new products to a quality community, increase the number of one's fans and followers, increase the number of leads by increasing the number of subscribers to a loyalty program or the number of downloads of an application, etc.

Clearly defining your objectives before setting out in search of influencers will enable you to rapidly and effectively evaluate if you have attained them post-action or post-campaign.

Step #02: judiciously select your influencers

Once your objectives are clearly defined, it is a question of identifying the most relevant influencers to promote your brand. Base this on five selection criteria:

- the size of their online community;

- the quality of their audience;

- their power of influence, their reputation and their emotional capital with the public;

- their level of activity;

- the quality of their content.

Next, start researching influencers who best match these criteria. The people you choose must have a certain level of fame and be immediately recognized by the consumers that you are trying to reach and convince through them. They must match the values of your brand in order to be credible when they promote it.

If you call on celebrities, make sure, during the creation of your campaigns, that your brand and not the celebrity is the star. Whatever celebrity you choose, he or she must embody the spirit of your brand, ideally in order to pass on the image of your brand and thus to avoid negative reactions from your audience, who will see nothing more than a publicity stunt.

Knowing that the most popular and/or active people on social media platforms are not necessarily those who have a quality audience, take care to select those who, beyond being strongly involved, are followed by fans and followers that represent true potential buyers for you. These are influencers who will be of great value for promoting your brand and, through their actions, winning over their whole community.

Step #03: make contact

Once the right influencers are identified, follow them on social media, like, comment and share their posts, etc. The objective of this step is to establish a first contact by showing your interest in them. By being regularly present among the active members of their community – which they will notice by looking at the notifications of those who have reacted to their posts – you will stand out among the many proposals they receive.

Then, contact them directly. To maximize your chances of getting a reaction from them, it is indispensable to personalize your message.

TURN YOUR BUSINESS INTO A RELATIONAL BRAND

WORD OF MOUTH FROM CUSTOMERS WHO ARE SATISFIED AND MAKE IT KNOWN IS WORTH ITS WEIGHT IN GOLD.

Delphine Lang

WWW.DELPHINELANG.COM

Once you have established direct contact, be patient if they do not respond immediately. The more popular and liked the influencers are on social media, the more brands reach out to them. Wait a few days, then try again.

A non-immediate reaction from them should not prevent you from maintaining the contact you have with them by continuing to follow their activities on social media. This naturally also holds true in the event an influencer agrees to enter into collaboration with you.

Step #04: find a collaboration formula that is profitable for everyone

Always keep in mind the ultimate goal of every collaboration with influencers: winning over their online communities through actions that they take to promote your brand and products. Consequently, write up a sufficiently attractive and convincing dossier in order to get a favorable response from them to your proposal for collaboration. In your dossier, take care to give them all the attention they deserve by showcasing them.

Apart from those who only act for purely commercial reasons, the majority of influencers promote brands they believe in. Whether you have selected brand ambassadors – those who have already lived the experience with your brand – or famous influencers – for whom that is not necessarily the case – every influencer is looking to live useful and enriching experiences and take pleasure in talking about their interests and passions with the Internet users who follow them on social media. It is therefore by always giving influencers more reasons to be interested in you through their immersion in the heart of your brand and through the customer experience you offer that they will be motivated and excited to engage in a constructive collaboration with you.

In order to clearly and effectively explain to them what you expect from them within the framework of an eventual future partnership, favor the organization of events during which you will present your brand, give influencers the opportunity to discover and test your products, and pass on the message that you want them to convey on the web. If you do not have the means, send your proposal by email and offer them the possibility of testing your new products for free by sending them samples or by giving them free access to your new services if that is what you market.

Once you have convinced certain influencers to collaborate with you and you have given them the message to pass on to their public, you must give them the full freedom necessary to enable them to make it their own easily and express themselves freely.

It is important that their messages remain authentic and credible, hence the necessity of respecting their ways of speaking. To maintain the trust of their fans and followers, they have to be honest and sincere, which means having total editorial liberty, even if this results in highlighting the defects and failures of your products. If this should happen to you and even if it is not what you were expecting, consider these opinions not as critiques, but more as avenues for improvement to take into consideration to optimize your products and services and to continually respond better to the needs and expectations of your customers.

It is through the sense of freedom that you will have given them that they will speak with pleasure and interest to their online community, in the own spaces of expressions, in their own way and with their own words – which should not stop you from setting them straight if they do not use appropriate terms to showcase the benefits of your products. The goal is to ensure a transfer of skills to the influencers, to give them a real role in order to motivate them.

Step #05: develop and maintain continuous relationships

To maintain and strengthen the involvement of your influencers continuously, it is essential to attach importance to them by highlighting the value they bring you through their recommendations and testimonials. Value them in the actions that you carry out on your own pages, accounts and/or channels.

If you want them to stay loyal to your brand, inform them before anyone else about launches of your new products, call on them again if the first collaboration has been fruitful, reward them for their loyalty, make them benefit from exclusive benefits, etc., in order to develop their sense of belonging to your community. It is equally important to give them the opportunity to talk amongst themselves and with your brand, to share their experiences, by clearly letting them know that you are completely available and ready to listen to them if necessary, while favoring direct encounters as much as possible.

Make sure that you are constantly developing and maintaining the trust-based relationships that you will have built with them. Your approach must above all be human-centered and you must put the right conditions in place in order to ensure the success of the actions undertaken.

Finally, reward them for their engagement. That is the guarantee of a fruitful partnership in the long term.

By establishing collaborations with relevant influencers and by proposing win-win exchanges, you will succeed in boosting your online reputation and promoting, on a larger scale, your brand and products.

Your community will then come to life itself and you will need to invest less and less in ad campaigns.

By immersing Internet users, your influencers included, at the heart of your brand through a value-creating offer and by always more providing them with useful and enriching solutions, you will succeed in building, maintaining and strengthening trust-based relationships with them. From then on, they will all be more inclined to talk about and bring your brand to life without you necessarily having to ask them.

Considering you as a valuable partner, they in turn will become valuable partners for your brand, which is unquestionably the best illustration of the power of a brand on social media and which will give you the absolute guarantee of sustainable and profitable growth of your activities.

In conclusion, it is always quality that brings customers to you. The value you will gain in the eyes of your public, by means of your actions and those of your best representatives – your customers – will unquestionably put you on the path to success.

It remains for me to thank you for your interest in discovering my approach.

Now that you possess the formula that will enable you to guarantee the success and profitability of your social media activities, get started... and especially and above all, believe in yourself and in your ability to create and implement your unique and differentiated strategy, which will allow you to stand out from your competitors and win over your customers.

Know that I will always be there for you on social networking sites. I invite you to visit my website www.delphinelang.com to find links to the different platforms.

I wish you all the success you deserve.

TURN YOUR BUSINESS INTO A RELATIONAL BRAND

**REFLECT THE IMAGE
OF A CONNECTED COMPANY
ABLE TO UNDERSTAND AND ANTICIPATE
THE SLIGHTEST EXPECTATION
OF YOUR CUSTOMERS.**

Delphine Lang

WWW.DELPHINELANG.COM

Acknowledgments

First of all, I would like to thank my mother, to whom I dedicate this book. My precious mother who is no longer by my side to share with me all of the incredible things that, for some time, I have been experiencing.

My mother, Dominique Lang, without whom I would not have become who I am today. A brilliant woman, a fighter, who always put others before herself.

My mother, who always believed in me more than I believed in myself and who so often told me she knew I would succeed. She remained by my side, supported and encouraged me, and for that, I thank her from the bottom of my heart.

She was my life, my rock, my "Mamouli d'amour." When she left us on March 4, 2013, taken by cancer after many long months during which she fought her last fight, I really believed I would not be able to go on. Without her. I told her this a few days before her passing, and she told me to fight, telling me that she knew I could do it. So I held on as hard as I could, in order to not disappoint her, but rather to make her proud. The goal in my line of sight, I made every effort to succeed. Long months of working relentlessly. Months of thinking, reflecting, creating, questioning my ideas, refining my deepest convictions and writing for weeks at a time to release this book, in order to pass on my knowledge and transform my dream into a reality: that of making my contribution to the world and helping others – you – to achieve your goals.

My mother never knew the success that she so deserved. So, if this book achieves the success I so hope for, it will be for her, and for me.

I hope that, in the place where she is now, she is proud of me.

Finally, I want to thank Jérôme de Bucquois, my guide for years, who has been at my side and has helped me in the right direction. He made me realize that I had incredible gifts that I was not exploiting. If he had not led me to this realization, I might have continued to waste my time, as I was so intent on doing. An operating mode that I knew only too well. A way of hurting myself to pay the price of the guilt that I felt, mistakenly, after a series of ordeals that I suffered without knowing how to defend myself against individuals that I thought stronger than me and who made me bear the much too heavy burden of their own responsibilities. Ordeals that leave scars for life. Certain ordeals that I got through with my mother by my side, both of us united and together, others that I had to overcome alone. I who, having always dreamed big and believed deep down that I would become what I had always dreamed of being, might never have arrived. However, instead of knocking me down, these ordeals made me stronger and gave me the desire to fight to fulfill the mission that I had given myself after the departure of my mother, in order to change what needs to be changed and contribute, in my way, to making the world a better place. Never the victim, always responsible.

Do we not say that those who have had a painful past are those who give everything they have to succeed? Well, I think I am one of those people. In a way, I thank those who have created obstacles for me because, in a way, without them, I would not be where I am now.

Whatever happened, my guide enabled me to pick myself up again. He never pushed me, but he challenged me. He is a great person, unmatched and amazing. I know that I can always count on him to find the energy and confidence that I sometimes lack in order to move forward and to take full advantage of every wonderful thing that comes my way. His support is worth more than gold. Many thanks to him.

I would also like to thank my editor, without whom this book would never have seen the light of day. Thank you for having believed in me and for having given me a chance to realize my dream of publishing this book.

Finally, thank you to all of you who are reading. You who follow perhaps me on social media. If so, know that your interest and engagement in the posts I have shared with you for some time is, for me, a source of incredible and incalculable energy. When I got started on social media – primarily Instagram – I was still in the process of writing. In seeing the impressive number of reactions and in reading your comments, it take a long time for me to realize that this could happen to me. And yet, it has. This helped confirm a little more that what I was doing, I had to finish to the end. For you, for me, and for the handful of people who believed in me. So that one day you could hold this book in your hands. You, without whom I would not be here.

Thank you so very much.

THE SOCIALKIND STRATEGIC BLUEPRINT

TURN YOUR BUSINESS INTO A RELATIONAL BRAND

① HOW TO THINK

LAY THE 7 PILLARS
OF AN IDEAL CULTURE

- #01 Responsibility
- #02 Engagement
- #03 Collaboration
- #04 Risk-taking
- #05 Innovation
- #06 Optimization
- #07 Optimism

② HOW TO BEHAVE

BUILD A POWERFUL
STRATEGY IN 10 STEPS

- #01 Clearly define your brand identity
- #02 Precisely set your objectives
- #03 Conduct a precise analysis of the competition
- #04 Acquire an in-depth understanding of your customers
- #05 Draw up a consistent offer that meets the demand
- #06 Set up your pages and accounts on the appropriate channels
- #07 Define key themes and create optimized content
- #08 Establish an editorial calendar
- #09 Implement a database of customer knowledge
- #10 Measure your performance and adjust your strategy

③ HOW TO ACT

ADOPT THE 12 BEST
FUNDAMENTAL PRACTICES

- #01 Use the codes specific to social media
- #02 Publish regularly and at the right time
- #03 Ensure constant monitoring
- #04 Deal with all requests
- #05 Listen attentively and empathetically
- #06 Respond quickly
- #07 Participate in discussions
- #08 Provide guidance and direction
- #09 Demonstrate transparency and sincerity
- #10 Calm things down and use private messages
- #11 Solicit influencers
- #12 Reward loyalty at two levels

Delphine Lang

WWW.DELPHINELANG.COM

Selective bibliography

1. "The Consumer Conversation – The experience void between brands and their customers", Econsultancy in association with IBM ExperienceOne. Study carried out in 276 companies and with 1,135 consumers in North America during the first quarter of 2015.

2. G.C. Kane, D. Palmer, A. N. Phillips, D. Kiron and N. Buckley, "Strategy, not Technology, Drives Digital Transformation", MIT Sloan Management Review-Deloitte University Press, July 2015. Study carried out in 4,800 companies in 129 countries and 27 activity sectors during the Fall of 2015.

3. N. G. Carr, "IT Doesn't Matter", Harvard Business Review, May 2003.

4. Anne Marie, *"Les besoins fondamentaux ou la pyramide Maslow"*, etats-d-esprit.com.

5. Segmentation marketing, *"Les critères de segmentation marketing"*, Analyse marketing.

www.LexitisEditions.fr

www.ingramcontent.com/pod-product-compliance
Lightning Source LLC
Chambersburg PA
CBHW080554220326
41599CB00032B/6476